SEARCH FOR SIGNIFICANCE

Finding Meaning in Times of Change, Challenge, and Chaos

Geri Marr Burdman, Ph.D.

Foreword by Sam Horn

SEARCH FOR SIGNIFICANCE

Finding Meaning in Times of Change, Challenge, and Chaos

Geri Marr Burdman, Ph.D.

FOREWORD BY SAM HORN

*B*ellevue *P*ress

A Division of GeroWise® International
www.gerowise.com
308 East Goodwin Street
Prescott, Arizona 86303 USA

Edited by Kate Robinson

Book and cover design by R. Burdman

ISBN 978-0-615-22238-7
Printed in the United States of America

To
Roberto
and
Our Global Family

CONTENTS

FOREWORD

No matter how busy, tired or overwhelmed you are, please make time for this book.

Keep it by your bed and read it before you go to sleep. It will put a smile in your heart and lead to peaceful dreams.

In the morning, dip into it for a few minutes before starting your day. It will remind you of what matters and send you on your way, calm and clear in your commitment to being the quality of person you want to be–no matter what.

If you are going through a tough time–if you're working or living with someone who doesn't appreciate you; if you're dealing with a health challenge or financial problems–this book will be a solace for your soul.

Search for Significance will center you in what counts. Remind you that it's making a difference for others that matters, not making a name, making a million, or making a mark.

If you find yourself feeling depressed, alone, or afraid, this book will serve as your companion. It will introduce you to other people who have survived challenging times. People who have gone on to lead meaningful lives full of joy and contribution, so you start believing again that you can too.

In a world that's full of headlines and news broadcasts focusing on man's inhumanity to man, we need books that showcase our infinite capacity to love one another and be humane. We need hope and evidence that we can and should be kind and compassionate.

This book offers that hope and evidence. Author Geri Marr Burdman, Ph.D. has been privileged to travel the world and meet fascinating people who have generously shared their hard-won wisdom. She herself is respected amongst her colleagues and clients for her life-affirming insights that have brought peace of mind to many.

Please set aside time for this book. It's the equivalent of setting aside time for yourself. Within these pages, you'll find answers to questions that human beings have been asking from the beginning of time.

1. How can I lead a purposeful life that matters?

2. How can I overcome adversity, recover from hurt and heartbreak, persevere through challenges, not give in to despair?

3. How can I be a quality person – even in the midst of chaos?

4. How can I live with grace, gratitude and joy? How can I be genuinely happy?

5. How can I focus on the present–instead of getting swept up in regrets or fears?

The author is a walking-talking role model of the principles she shares in this book. She writes with such integrity. Her honesty and heart shine through. I can't imagine anyone reading this book and not being powerfully, positively impacted. Read it and reap . . . and share it with your loved ones so they too can benefit from these insights.

Sam Horn, June 19, 2008

INTRODUCTION

On a sultry September afternoon in 1968, I was sipping a mango-flavored ice cone while walking to my next class at the University of Puerto Rico. I paused briefly to glance at some ads on a cluttered bulletin board in the hallway. Among "rooms for rent," "rides to Ponce" and a swarm of other announcements, a hand-written note leapt out at me. It said:

Dr. Viktor Frankl
Holocaust survivor, founder of Logotherapy, the third Viennese school of psychotherapy, presenting a seminar for faculty and graduate students
TODAY AT FOUR PM

I had not heard of Viktor Frankl nor of Logotherapy, though I was a counseling graduate student at the time. I liked reading about the works of Sigmund Freud, Alfred Adler and others, so I went to hear what this man from Vienna, Frankl, had to say.

As I entered that seminar, little did I know that I was about to experience a life-changing event. When the bespectacled, agile, sixty-three year old Viktor Frankl took the podium, a hush came over the room. Without hesitation he began speaking in a serene, firm voice about his life's work and the unspeakable suffering he and his loved ones had endured at the hands of the Nazis. Viktor Frankl's wife, mother, father, brother, sister-in-law, and mother-in-law along with six million Jews and fifteen million others—perished in the concentration camps.

I learned that Viktor Frankl had documented his experiences of the concentration camps in his classic book *Man's Search for Meaning*. First published in 1946 and now in its 73rd printing, Frankl's book has been translated into over 25 languages, and it has been listed by the U.S. Library of Congress as one of the ten most influential books in print.

I was struck by the absolute absence of bitterness in Viktor Frankl's voice and demeanor. When he quoted the words of Frederick Nietzsche, "He who has a why to live can endure almost any how," I was moved to start taking notes on how Frankl's work reflected his own heartrending experiences.

Viktor Frankl explained that as a psychiatrist and neurologist, he was already writing and lecturing on Logotherapy before World War II. Then he spoke of having studied extensively with Sigmund Freud and Alfred Adler, founders of two Viennese schools of psychotherapy of the era. Frankl went on to say that while he respected his teachers greatly, early on he began to differentiate his philosophy and psychology from theirs.

What really caught my attention that September day was Frankl's unwavering conviction that humans are not merely destined to "pursue pleasure" as Freud's followers believed or to "pursue power" as Adler proposed. There is a greater motivating force behind all human behavior and that is the "pursuit of meaning," Viktor Frankl taught. He indicated that seeking meaning is much more than the pursuit of success or happiness—"these must come as by-products!"

I became increasingly intrigued with Frankl's unique approach to looking at humanhood when he began to address our individual responsibility to others and to the world. Reflecting on his experiences, Frankl passionately told us that humans have a capacity to suffer courageously—even to bring good out of unavoidable adversity. He insisted:

"The ability to choose one's attitude toward any situation is irrevocable."

Dr. Frankl said that we create meaning through our actions as we move through life. As he left the ornately carved mahogany podium, he moved deliberately forward. He paused and asked us "to ponder deeply how we discover meaning with each new day."

When Viktor Frankl came to speak in Puerto Rico, I had been living on that tropical island for about three years. After working in Sucre, Bolivia as a Peace Corps volunteer in the early 1960s, I continued seeking opportunities for change and challenge through global health work.

I fell in love with the generous spirit of the Puerto Rican people as I worked with community health programs throughout the island. I had just embarked on graduate studies in counseling when I came across that hastily handwritten bulletin board notice. I felt a strong nudge to attend—no doubt about it. But I still had no idea of the impactful lesson that I was about to receive.

5

Viktor Frankl left an indelible imprint on my soul. Deeply moved by his wisdom and compassion, I can still feel the resonance of the moment when he exhorted us to:

**"Listen to the person on the street;
he or she will be your teacher!"**

I remember feeling a deep sense of recognition in his powerful message, unlike any I had heard before. After his seminar, I just wanted to sit in silence. I made a beeline across campus to a tiny alcove laden with hibiscus plants near the library to ponder the experience. It was a transformative moment. And I jotted a note to myself: **"Take time, listen, who are your teachers?"**

My journey from that day forward has been to listen, to learn, and to share the wisdom of teachers I encounter along the way. Work assignments have taken me to many parts of the globe including Africa, Latin America, Asia, Australia, New Zealand, and the Caribbean.

The greatest teachers can be found in the most unlikely situations and circumstances. Many are quietly sharing their wisdom through their daily actions.

The world over, people are seeking to understand: What's it all about? What am I here for? Why me? Why now? What next?

Have you asked yourself any of these questions? I invite you to explore them and map your path toward a more purposeful life, even in the midst of the changes, challenges, and chaos that may be swirling all around you.

Lessons I learned from Viktor Frankl and other

visionaries and mentors I have met on my journey are featured in each chapter of this book. I've shared insights from timeless philosophers, clients, colleagues and my own experiences with the hope that you, too, will embark upon a "Search for Significance" regardless of what is happening in your life today. May you discover your path to wholeness and build the meaning- filled life that you deserve!

CHAPTER ONE

A Path With Heart:
Finding Your Inner Compass in the Midst of Caregiving

LOOK TO THIS DAY

Look to this day,
For it is life,
The very life of life.
In its brief course lie all
The realities and truths of existence,
The joy of growth,
The splendor of action,
The glory of power.
For yesterday is but a dream
And tomorrow is only a vision.
But today, well lived,
Makes every yesterday
A memory of happiness
And every tomorrow a vision of hope.
Look well, therefore, to this day.

Sanskrit Proverb

I frequently open my seminars by reading the ancient Sanskrit verse "Look to this Day." Then I invite participants, often of all ages and backgrounds, to momentarily leave their cares at the door and focus on the words.

Upon hearing the Sanskrit verse at a recent seminar, Patricia, a tall, slender fifty-five-year old high school teacher and community activist introduced herself. And then she spoke of her challenges as sole caregiver for her eighty-year old widowed mother who suffers from dementia.

Patricia told us that her mother, a librarian and leader in her coastal Oregon community had experienced several "mini-strokes" shortly after the death of her husband just two years ago. Patricia went on to explain, "At first Mom's symptoms were relatively minor, occasional forgetfulness and slight difficulty forming sentences. But Mom remained active and loved her book club!" "About a year ago," Patricia continued "friends and neighbors began calling me, concerned that Mom wasn't taking care of herself."

Friends began telling Patricia that her mother rarely left the house and refused to participate in her beloved book club and, most alarming, did not seem to recognize people she had known for years. When the calls started coming with increasing urgency, Patricia, an only child, consulted her mother's doctor and immediately closed the family home on the coast and moved her mother to live with her near Portland, Oregon.

Patricia described her life as "a juggling act on constant alert." Another participant, John, asked Patricia, "How do you cope?"

Patricia responded, "I try to remember that life is calling—calling me to be authentic—nothing more, nothing less."

A profound silence enveloped the room! Patricia's story reminded us that finding meaning in such a situation could be an invitation to discover our inner compass.

A lively discussion ensued about the sensation of being lost in the midst of caregiving responsibilities. "Rudderlessness," said John, "is hard to face."

Have you found yourself feeling lost in the maze of caregiving? Feeling overwhelmed? Not knowing where to turn?

Confronting Life's Challenges

Learning to confront challenges and to understand the process of growth through life's transition experiences can a powerful springboard to a *meaning-filled* life regardless of circumstances. I am convinced that we are called to map a route to nurture ourselves, especially at times when we are focused on caring for others.

Population aging is one of the prominent markers of our times. A person plucked from the first half of the twentieth century and dropped into today's world would be struck by the sheer number of mid-life and older persons—and by their visibility and imprint on society. The undeniable impact of seventy-five million "boomers" is a constant reminder of our changing landscape.

As the ravages of time are affecting the people who raised our boomer generation, the sons and daughters like Patricia are frequently required to shoulder what is all too often called a "burden" of care. Throughout the world, aging populations are enlisting more and more of us to be caregivers and care partners.

Indeed caregiving has become an integral part of millions of boomers' lives even as they hold down full-time jobs. Often referred to as the "sandwich generation" many boomers are caught in the middle of parent care while their own children and, in some cases, grandchildren still require attention, energy, and resources.

Caregivers—men as well as women—face enormous challenges juggling responsibilities with employment and other daily demands. We are being stretched emotionally, physically, and financially in ways we never imagined possible.

Many caregivers experience physical as well as emotional maladies (including depression and despair) while in the process of caring for significant others, especially parents and spouses. The general consensus is that we caregivers are on perilous ground.

The truth is that most of us are woefully unprepared for these multiple obligations. And neither our academic achievements nor even our experience in the professional caregiving arena can mitigate our lack of preparedness.

Navigating Uncharted Waters

My clients frequently tell me about the myriad of emotions they experience. Fatigue and clouded judgment take a huge toll as they attempt to navigate the uncharted waters of caregiving.

Have you noticed that dilemmas posed by boomers' challenges are a recurrent theme in the media today? Magazines, newspapers, and television programs remind us almost daily of the intimidating challenges and their effects on us caregivers. Yet we hardly know where to turn for guidance when we need it most.

Just how ill-equipped I was for the stresses and rollercoaster emotions that are an integral part of a caregiver's journey became exceedingly clear to me in recent years as I was personally tested to "walk my talk." As a health counseling and gerontology specialist, I have given seminars, taught university and community-based courses, consulted in many parts of the world, as well as written a college textbook on how to improve quality of life in later years.

I had lots of answers! But, alas, for a good part of the past decade I found myself in the role of caregiver for my mother and two aunts as they navigated their final stages of life.

These fiercely independent women taught me more than I could have imagined as each of them experienced enormous health challenges. Above all, they taught me the importance of deep listening and being present in the moment.

Caregiving demands also brought me intense

feelings of fatigue, rejection, despair, self doubt, and denial. The days and nights were sometimes indistinguishable.

My anguish was precisely what I had so often heard described by innumerable caregivers whom I had counseled. "Why me?" I thought some days, while other days I resolved silently "I will not succumb; I can do this!"

Why me?—Why not me? How could one day be so hopeful and the next so filled with self doubt and despair? Why was I isolating myself? What next? Where could I go for help?

Of course I knew I could consult the literature in my library and on the internet. While there is an abundance of advice on caregiving, at that vulnerable personal time I found that generally the guidelines were very matter-of-fact (i.e. *Get on with your life, caregiver*). Most tend to advise along the lines of recognizing and prioritizing problems; managing emotions; building partnerships with health and social service providers; balancing needs and resources; and taking charge in times of crisis.

While some guidelines do provide clear and straightforward formulas for caregivers, there is no "one size fits all." **Our emotional responses are highly variable.** Fortunately there are ever increasing numbers of community support groups that provide assistance and invaluable lifelines for caregivers of all ages in the midst of seemingly overwhelming responsibilities.

What About Managing Our Emotions?

What about managing those emotions? I plumbed the depths of my soul for messages that resonated for me. I had encountered many teachers along the way, but it was Viktor Frankl's work that impacted every fiber of my being. How might I apply lessons I learned from Dr. Frankl now that I was facing daily challenges shared by innumerable other caregivers?

How might I distill and apply the wisdom of one of the most significant influences of my life? And how could I share the essence of Dr. Viktor Frankl's Logotherapy so that others might find solace, inspiration, and even opportunity for growth while in their own quagmire?

I have come to believe that we are called to look beyond appearances, to actually thrive rather than merely survive caregiving challenges. Unlocking our potential for "soulful" freedom in the midst of caregiving, regardless of the circumstances, becomes a daily challenge.

Can we banish the word "burden" from our vocabulary? Can we transform our caregiving responsibilities to a vehicle for growth? Can we draw upon caregiving challenges as an opportunity for deeper understanding of our inner selves and our place in the wheel of life?

Caregiving permeates all aspects of life: emotional, physical, and spiritual. Its multiple facets affect our identities, beliefs, hopes, and dreams. Invariably, unresolved issues surface and often the "fatigue factor" colors everything a hazy grey.

Staying Afloat

I liken caregiving to treading water around the clock, surrounded by strong currents that test our ability to remain afloat. We caregivers know that unreasonable things happen; that our life, along with that of our loved one, is changing forever. Some days, staying afloat is about all we can hope for.

When I described my caregiving challenges at a workshop in San Francisco, Leslie, a banking executive stood up and startled me with her insightful comment: "float is what it's all about, Geri! In fact," Leslie continued, "a basic water survival technique is to put your head back and look up . . . " That caught our attention! I later learned that Leslie, in addition to her day job, also gives swimming lessons in her community.

Have you ever felt that you were being pulled under by the tide? What current is pulling you down? Do you recall learning to float?

I remember an instructor who taught me to swim when I was about twelve: *Float—or you will be exhausted and you will go under!* I had not thought of that lesson until Leslie reminded us of a timeless survival technique: **"Relax, head back, look up!"**

Balance in the Midst of Change

Recently I was invited to give a seminar on Caregiving Challenges for the staff at a Veterans Administration Medical Center in the Southwest. In response to the invitation, I sent the organizer my title: "Maintaining and Sustaining Balance in the

Midst of Change." When I arrived to give the seminar, the word "Midst" had been changed to "Mist"
on the printed programs. What a sublime misprint!

We seized the moment to grapple with the participants' realities as caregiving professionals and family
members alike. After a lively discussion we concluded that caregiving sometimes feels like being in
a dark mist over uncharted waters. But, we were reminded that day by Ursula, a quiet unassuming
nursing assistant who had listened intently to the
discussion, that the Navajo have a saying:

**"Out of the deep dark mist there is a rainbow
trail."**

We know conditions that require caregiving de-
rive from mental as well as physical changes in our
loved ones. Yet it is hard to accept that changes in
personality and behavior are often a direct result of
brain dysfunction such as dementia. We caregivers
can be devastated and frightened beyond belief by
the very nature of our changing relationships, especially in parent-son or daughter interactions and in
spousal relationships.

Caregivers of spouses discover that the partnership is drastically altered. Roles, expectations, social
activities, intimacy, and communication are all affected. Often a host of unwelcome emotions
emerges, sometimes concurrently; fear, frustration,
anger, despair, sadness, and loneliness are all part of
the package.

Depression is a common occurrence. Feelings of intense sadness, hopelessness, irritability, and sleep dis-

turbances signal a need for medical treatment and should not be ignored.

The importance of self-care is not readily evident to many caregivers. Amid the stresses of a multitude of responsibilities, it is all too easy to overlook, or simply lack the time or energy to acknowledge, that we are suffering from exhaustion and sleep deprivation.

Dealing with Compassion Fatigue

Overwhelming emotions are sometimes called compassion fatigue or burnout. It is precisely the pressures on our time and energies—emotional as well as physical—that make self-care so vitally important.

Whenever I mention that I am involved with gerontology and caregiving, people invariably respond with their personal stories. This response occurs irrespective of where I am, be it on airplanes, at meetings with colleagues, with neighbors, or at community events. The caregiver stories I hear are often heartrending: stories of loneliness, family dissention, grief, fear, bewilderment.

Feelings of entrapment are rampant. Where to turn? What to do? The circumstances are as unique as fingerprints, and no path is set out for any of us.

The words of the Spanish poet Antonio Machado often come to mind:

"Caminante, no hay camino. Se hace camino al andar . . ." — "Sojourner, there is no path; you make your path by walking . . . "

Navigating the Unknown

I have come to believe that creating a path is an invitation to discover our inner compass. Navigating the unknown as a caregiver in recent years, my greatest solace came from the teachings of Viktor Frankl. Again and again I recalled how his life work focused on helping people find meaning in their own lives regardless of circumstance, age or social condition. He referred to giving as a way of being!

In the concentration camps, Viktor Frankl lost everything and everyone near and dear to him: his wife, his family, his written works—and nearly his life. Throughout the horrendous travails of those years, he was sustained by a vision and passion to share a message of hope with the world. And subsequently he indeed traveled the world teaching and living his passion.

Never forget, Viktor Frankl taught,

" . . . we find meaning in life even when facing a fate that cannot be changed— when confronted with a seemingly hopeless situation. When we are no longer able to change a situation, we are ultimately challenged to change ourselves."

Search for Meaning

The search for meaning is a universal longing among humans. The meaning of life differs from person to person, from day to day, from hour to hour. What matters, above all, is the specific meaning we choose at any given moment. And the choice is always ours!

Meaning is experienced by responding to the demands of any situation at hand, discovering and making a commitment to our own unique task. Caregiving in today's uncertain world often challenges us to create, as we go, a path through the unknown.

Compassion fatigue, burnout, caregiver fatigue—all are common symptoms of our times. They can generate a sense of estrangement or abandonment, of not belonging, of not knowing where to turn. Feelings of meaninglessness or inner emptiness take a huge toll on health as well as quality of our lives. One of the great imperatives for caregivers is to realize: **I am not alone.**

Our choices and, above all, our attitudes season the unfolding chapters of our lives. We are all compositions in progress, growing and realizing our potential day by day. As we learn to listen within, our inner compass becomes more accessible. Learning to read that compass—and to refine our listening skills leads to new dimensions of inner healing.

Remembering that the journey is taken one day at a time helps keep a perspective. In the next chapters we will explore essential elements of our universal *"Search for Significance."*

CHAPTER TWO

Tears in the Rain:
Dealing with Despair

Walk on a rainbow trail;
Walk on a trail of song,
And all about you will be beauty.
There is a way out of every dark mist,
Over a rainbow trail.

Navajo Song

Behind every adversity lies a hidden
possibility.

Sufi Proverb

In the midst of winter, I discovered
that there is within me an Invincible
Summer.

A. Camus

Recently I was invited to speak at a community forum in Arizona on the topic **"Finding Meaning throughout the Lifespan."** Prescott and Sedona, high desert towns in Yavapai County, Arizona touted by tourism magazines as among the best places to retire in the USA, have a high incidence of depression and elder suicide despite material affluence. Many who choose to live in these communities come from highly successful careers and abundant life experiences (movie industry executives, bankers, CEOs of Fortune 500 companies, to name a few).

But the area is no golden land of rich retirees, either. There are young families struggling to keep afloat as well as a burgeoning of retirees living only on social security. Economic disparities are seen throughout the region. And depression is an equal opportunity malady.

But why is depression and despair so prevalent? What are people going through? Is there some gnawing inner emptiness? Are there antidotes for despair?

As I began to speak, a searing question was posed by a sprightly silver-haired woman seated in the front row: "Dr. Marr Burdman, let's cut to the chase —what can we do about this problem of despair that we are all hearing about these days?" I promised to try to lay out some stepping stones and share with them the essence of Viktor Frankl's message:

The search for purpose and meaning is a universal longing. It is our deepest need to make sense of our lives even in the midst of chaos and change—and, yes, even in despair.

An Imperative of Our Times

I mentioned the World Health Organization's definition of health: "a state of physical, mental and social well-being and not merely the absence of disease." The spiritual dimension is often added to this definition. Indigenous people around the globe are teaching us about the interrelationship of mind, body, spirit—Wisdom of the Ages.

Will we listen? I believe we are called to listen deeply; it is an imperative of our times.

For the past couple of centuries, depression, or melancholy as it was once called, has figured prominently in the lives of such noteworthy individuals as the Russian novelist Leo Tolstoy, German social scientist Max Weber, American psychologist William James, English playwright and essayist Samuel Johnson, among many others. Indeed the condition called depression grew in prevalence over the course of the twentieth century and has now increased to pandemic proportions.

According to the World Health Organization, depression is the fifth leading cause of death and disability in the world. Mortality occurs, of course, through suicide. But even a milder form of depression—termed dysthemia and characterized by an inability to experience pleasure—can lead to morbidity and mortality through increasing a person's vulnerability to serious illness such as cancers and heart ailments. This malady strikes all levels of society and both women and men. And all ages!

In recent years voluminous books, articles, and

media presentations have focused on the toll of depression in the workplace, in the home, and in society at large. The roles of gender, genetic factors, and pharmacological and counseling interventions are subjects of continuous study. And the use of medication in treatment and management of depression is certainly on the forefront with increasing evidence of efficacy.

Back to the question posed at the community forum in Arizona: "Why are despair and suicide so prevalent in our communities?"

That question brought forth an almost unanimous audience response that I consider only part of the answer. They said:"Because people don't have good support networks; they are disconnected from family and friends; distant from that which gives them grounding."

And then the participants began to share stories of their neighbors and the widowed folk in their grand homes no longer able to drive and distant from relatives after the death of a spouse. Of course, we were reminded of the other part of the picture. We have to look at the proportion of older persons in these rapidly growing communities. Sometimes the problems seem more dramatic simply because the numbers are greater. But the problem is huge!

I asked how many of the group had heard of Viktor Frankl. When I mentioned the book: *Man's Search for Meaning*, a few hands went up in recognition. When I stated that Viktor Frankl continues to be one of my greatest teachers, I experienced a palpable spark of curiosity in the audience.

Each of us, as we look back over our lifetime, recognize that there have been teachers who planted seeds and helped put us on a path that led to who we are today. Our paths are unique and each of us has specific assignments.

Viktor Frankl awakened me to my personal path and the work that was to come. When I met him at the University of Puerto Rico decades ago, I knew absolutely nothing of his story. But the profound impact of that encounter was a defining moment in my life.

Teachers and Way-Showers

We all have had encounters with people along the way who helped to shape our lives. Think about your own life. Who have been those way-showers for you? Did you recognize their impact at the time?

Many of us recognize such significant experiences only in retrospect.

When we take time to reflect, we often recognize pivotal events that have shaped our destiny. Can you think of a particular event or person that touched you deeply? How was that for you?

In a nutshell, I'll describe the essence of the lessons I received from Viktor Frankl, a message he shared as he traveled around the globe.

You may recall that Frankl's message differs greatly from that of Sigmund Freud and Alfred Adler. Freud said that the motivating force behind all human behavior is *a will to pleasure.*

Adler said what motivates human behavior is *a will to power,* a will to have dominion over other people and that's what keeps us going—a spirit of competition, a will to win, a will to dominate.

Viktor Frankl held that the motivating force behind human behavior is *a will to meaning*. When people have a reason to get out of bed in the morning or a purpose in their lives, that pursuit of meaning propels them forward.

In my global work, I have seen Frankl's work validated innumerable times by the **"person in the street"** as he called those who are our **"real teachers."**

I, too, believe that the search for purpose and meaning is a primary motivating force behind humans the world over. I call it a *Search for Significance*: **What am I here for? What is my task? What is my assignment for this day? Why me? Why not me?**

Indeed, what kept Frankl alive through his immeasurable loss and trauma in the concentration camps was his vision that, if he survived, he would share this message with the world. He would demonstrate that there are antidotes to despair. There is a basic motivational force behind all human behavior—a pursuit of meaning or purpose regardless of circumstances.

Though his manuscript was confiscated and destroyed by guards at the concentration camp where he was imprisoned, Viktor Frankl managed to reconstruct on bits and pieces of paper the essence of his message. When he was miraculously released, very near death, Frankl re-drafted a manuscript that eventually led to the publication of his still-popular book *Man's Search for Meaning*.

An Antidote to Despair

Frankl's wisdom has reverberated around the world and is especially relevant to today's questions. Why is there so much despair? Why are we encountering so much pain in our midst and what can we do about it?

Frankl spoke of alienation—that sense of estrangement or abandonment, of not belonging. He characterized alienation as loss of interest and lack of initiative, attributing these to an "existential vacuum"—a feeling of meaninglessness or inner emptiness. For many this manifests in boredom or total lack of ability to experience pleasure.

Have you experienced that feeling of "not belonging?" I sometimes hear clients and friends say "everything is so difficult—I feel as if I am on another planet." What finally moves people to seek help is often this utterly painful feeling of disconnection.

In today's world, this alienation or existential vacuum takes a great toll among all age groups but especially among adolescents and elders. Frankl's Logotherapy holds that a search for meaning is the most significant motivational factor. It is an all-encompassing phenomenon of being human—reaching out for a meaning to fulfill or being connected to something or someone other than oneself.

Look to This Day for it is Life

People who seem to be the happiest and healthiest at any age are those who have a sense of community. These people are connected with others by mutual need, have a sense of identity, know themselves, and respect themselves. They strive for a purpose in their lives. They are active, engaged in something that gives them a reason to get out of bed and organize the day.

Yet, even the most actively engaged individuals experience periodic episodes of "down time" when questions loom: "Is it all worth it?" "Am I just spinning my wheels?" "What is this all about?" "What am I here for?"

I sometimes hear clients say, "Who would miss me if I didn't show up?" or "Is it really worth my effort?" Have you ever asked yourself any of these questions?

Have you ever awakened with a sensation of dread? Ever had that feeling of not knowing how to even begin to cope with the demands on your life? Have you ever felt like pulling the blankets over your head and staying put? Ever felt that you just could not face the day? You are not alone.

When you awaken overwhelmed with that sense of dread, is it possible to reframe and focus on This Day? What holds you back?

In my own daily *Search for Significance* I look for a *SIGN*. I have found four essential elements for setting my intention one day at a time. Therein lies the secret to *managing those emotions!* I invite you to look for your *SIGN*, just for *TODAY*.

S—Sign on, just for *Today.* Commit to living this day as it unfolds with all its change, challenge, and yes, even chaos. Be a participant observer. Watch the watcher, You! Remember, it is just for *TODAY.*

I—Invest in this Day. Focus on what is at hand. That is what you are called to do. Be open to whatever presents itself. Just for *TODAY.*

G—Go within and listen deeply. Within that well of Silence lie answers that are uniquely yours. You do not even need to ask the questions. Listen deeply. Just for *TODAY.*

N—Neutralize negativity. Promise yourself just for *TODAY* that you will park in neutral any and all of the resentments and negative emotions that came your way yesterday. No other action is required. You just will not entertain those feelings this day. Just for *TODAY.*

Activate Your Heart of Compassion

Your pain is the breaking of the shell that encloses your understanding. Even as the stone of the fruit must break, that its heart may stand in the sun, so must you know pain.

Kahlil Gibran

If we are to look for signs of significance in our lives, it is essential to recognize that the absence of despair is not what we seek. Rather, it may be that through the depth of despair we are able to realize our greatest potential. Emerging from the existential vacuum can activate a heart of compassion and deep understanding that moves us forward with purpose and passion.

How can this be? What insights have you gleaned from some of your most challenging times? How did you push through the pain?

Viktor Frankl's prescription for finding meaning regardless of outer circumstances is profound in its simplicity and has three tenets:

- *Doing a Deed*–This refers to accomplishment deemed of personal value and set as a goal. An example is community service. Reaching out and helping another.
- *Loving/Experiencing a Value*–Gaining full awareness of another, such as a work of art, nature, or a person—through love. Love is also experienced as a sense of connectedness with all that is. It is a profound sense of *Being One with the All*—a transcendental experience of *Oneness*.

- *Suffering*—When one has to face a fate that cannot be changed (loss of family, friends, work, or other serious loss, for example, an incurable illness) one is given an ultimate opportunity to actualize the highest value, to fulfill the deepest meaning—the meaning of suffering. What matters, above all, is the attitude one takes toward suffering—how we accept life circumstances.

Unconditional Meaningfulness

Viktor Frankl taught me to look at the *unconditional* meaningfulness of life. Sometimes it feels like we are surrounded by darkness and we doubt we'll ever move beyond the emotional pain. At these times it is essential to remember we are not alone. Seek out comfort from family, friends, and neighbors—or volunteer to help someone else in need.

I remember a day last July when I was so filled with intense grief over the death of a dear friend coupled with a series of other emotionally painful challenges that I wanted nothing to do with anyone. The last thing I wanted to do was pick up the phone and call someone. Yet after several days of self-imposed isolation, when I did reach out for help from a friend—a listening ear—I discovered that my unrelenting sense of sadness began to lift. And I realized I had allowed my friend to be a comforter. Friendship is a two way street—a reciprocal process.

Another source of solace I find is keeping a candle at my desk. I light it often, and take a silent pause, as a symbol that light endures—no matter what the circumstances. I also have a stained glass "inspiration box" filled with axioms and articles and letters that inspire me. When in doubt or pain, I like to go to that box that contains reminders to shift my attitude. I remember Frankl's words:

"When faced with a situation that cannot be changed, we are ultimately challenged to change ourselves."

Hope is the thing with feathers that perches in the soul and sings the tune without words and never stops at all.

Emily Dickinson

You give but little when you give of your possessions. It is when you give of yourself that you truly give.

Kahlil Gibran

CHAPTER THREE

Keys to Freedom:
Choosing Forgiveness

The practice of forgiveness is our most important contribution to the healing of the world.

Marianne Williamson

To forgive is to set a prisoner free and to discover the prisoner was you.

Lewis Smedes

Let every step I take be one of forgiveness.

Gerald Jampolsky

Forgiveness has many faces. There is the photo of Pope Paul II sitting in the jail cell with the man who tried to assassinate him. There are the news accounts of the Amish community in Pennsylvania extending a helping hand to the widow of the man who slaughtered their sons and daughters in a classroom one tranquil autumn day a few years ago. There is the quiet acceptance by the widow of a professor at Virginia Tech, slain while he helped his students escape through a window as he held the door against a crazed gunman intent on murdering anyone in sight.

When I heard Azim Khamisa speak just a few years ago of his 20-year old son, Tariq, who was murdered by a 14-year old gang member recruit in California, I was astounded by yet another account of tragedy turned into a powerful commitment to service. Khamisa's dedication in remembrance of his beloved son touched me deeply.

Mr. Khamisa, a handsome articulate man of Middle Eastern descent, shared his newfound life purpose at a Peace Alliance meeting in Washington, D.C. He also spoke about the intensity of his grief and that of Tariq's mother when they heard the news. Azim said the heart-wrenching shriek on the other end of the phone line when he called Tariq's mother is forever embedded in his memory.

Azim was astonished at his own response. Even in the midst of intense grief, he did not demand the usual revenge and retribution. Instead, he saw two of America's sons lost—one to death and one to the state prison system:

"From the outset, I saw victims on both ends of the gun. I will mourn Tariq's death for the rest of my life. Now, however, my grief has been transformed into a powerful commitment to change. Change is urgently needed in a society where children kill children."

Even more astonishing is that Azim Khamisa sought collaboration and forged a deep friendship with the murderer's grandfather. They work hand-in-hand to provide violence prevention education programs for young people. Azim established the *Tariq Khamisa Foundation* for the purpose of cultivating and nurturing a generation of peacemakers who will create a world free from youth violence.

There are countless other stories of acts of forgiveness, large and small, that are making a difference in today's world. *The Forgiveness Project—* backed by peacemakers including Archbishop Desmond Tutu—was started as a touring exhibition in 2004 to spread stories of peace instead of war.

Fredric Luskin, author of *Forgive for Good,* began his groundbreaking work on forgiveness as a graduate student at Stanford University. He has taken the concept and indeed the act of forgiveness to new levels. Forgiveness has become the subject of serious academic research through the Stanford Forgiveness Project and other educational institutions.

In his writing, Luskin lays out a pathway toward forgiveness that has generated interest and debate among academic colleagues and the public at large. The essence of the message I get from Luskin's work is simply stated:

"Forgiveness defuses anger and opens a dialogue for improved relationships. Even if the pain is impossible to for-

get, forgiveness liberates the soul."

What allowed Viktor Frankl to move through the world with his message of finding purpose in every day and every experience? How did he and countless others manage to forgive the unforgivable? What permitted him to deliver such a powerful and peaceful missive? The central theme of his work and life was forgiveness and purposefulness. How was that possible?

How have innocent victims of violence and injustice in myriad forms managed to forgive, let go, and move on? What is the attribute that permits the release of resentment? Have you pondered these questions?

"Forgiveness does not change the past, but it does enlarge the future."

Paul Boese

A Sure Remedy

While going through papers and sundry items left by my mother when she passed away several years ago, I came upon a writing that Mother had marked "Very important!" *A Sure Remedy* by Charles Fillmore gave a prescription for forgiveness. Fillmore suggested:

"Sit for half an hour every night and mentally forgive everyone against whom you have any ill will or antipathy. If you fear or if you are prejudiced against even an animal, mentally

38

ask forgiveness of it and send it thoughts of love. If you have accused anyone of injustice, if you have discussed anyone unkindly, if you have criticized or gossiped about anyone, withdraw your words by asking in the silence for forgiveness.
If you have had a falling out with friends or relatives, see all things and all persons as they really are—pure Spirit—and send them your strongest thoughts of love. Be patient, loving and kind, under all circumstances."

Now, my mother's family, and her generation for that matter, did not speak often of their beliefs or inner life. But it became clearer to me as I went through Mother's papers that she too was on a *Search for Significance*, especially in her later years. The markings on that well-worn sheet of paper about forgiveness tell me that Mother sought peace and solace in those words. And I know she tried to live them.

Forgiveness is at the Heart of Healing

In today's world, the very idea of forgiveness is repugnant to many who live by **"an eye for an eye and a tooth for a tooth."** Ghandi is said to have countered these words with: **"If we live by an eye for an eye and a tooth for a tooth . . . soon we will all be blind and toothless."**
Have we been blinded by our urge to get even? What allows some to let go while others only grow more embittered? I have known people whose resentments have virtually destroyed their lives. And

yet others have pushed through the painful experiences to new dimensions of living. What is the vehicle that permits such a breakthrough for some?

A few years ago my dear friend, Louise, and her husband were returning home from a dinner celebrating her 51st birthday when a drunken driver careened across the highway and hit their car head on. Paramedics were on the scene almost immediately and Louise was taken by ambulance to Harborview, a world-class trauma center in Seattle. Louise was placed on life support for several days before she died of severe head injuries resulting from the crash.

I remember vividly the sight of my dear friend bound in bandages and surrounded by machines in that intensive care unit. Her husband, Dave, was consumed with rage. Rage at the young man who was driving while intoxicated and who had escaped injury in the accident. Dave's thoughts were of revenge and, in his grief, he spoke of nothing else: "I'll get back at the guy who killed Louise!"

After months of deep grief and profuse anger, Dave had a remarkable change of heart. What prompted it? He could not explain except to say: "Louise held a light that kept me from stumbling. Now I need to hold that light." And Dave immersed himself in community work with Mothers Against Drunk Driving. He set about volunteering his services with community education campaigns and helping others heal their grief. To this day, Dave's pain from the loss of his beloved Louise is immense, but he was liberated from the unrelenting angst of unforgiveness.

What experiences in your life have shaped your attitudes toward forgiveness? Are there circumstances that seem totally unforgivable? Do we become imprisoned in our thoughts of unforgiveness?

All of us can read lofty words of forgiveness and repeat them but to live by the lessons is quite another story. Certainly I remember many times when I felt it impossible to let go of resentments. And I ruminated over and over the actions and inactions of others that led to those agonizing and relentless feelings.

Over the years in my *Search for Significance*, I have come to recognize that difficult as it may seem, forgiveness is at the heart of healing. Indeed, forgiveness is the key.

As my friend and wise teacher, Virginia Stephenson, has reminded me, "Forgiveness releases the baggage of the past and lifts the burdens of resentment and remorse. When we are mentally free of these emotions, love walks in with peace and good will."

CHAPTER FOUR

Life Review:
Discovering Meaning
Across the Lifespan

We shall not cease from exploration
And the end of all our exploring
Will be to arrive where we started
And know the place for the first time.

T. S. Eliot

Stories are medicine... They have such
power; they do not require that we do,
be, act anything—we need only listen.

Clarissa Pinkola Estes

When we listen we breathe in each
other's words.

Maxine Hong-Kinston

Becoming All We Can Be

Blanca Irizarry, Director of the Counseling Program at the University of Puerto Rico, introduced me to the relevance of Abraham Maslow's work to the field of rehabilitation counseling at the same time I met Dr. Viktor Frankl. Professor Irizarry, whose friendship I shall always treasure, reminded me that the essence of counseling is helping people to "be all they can be regardless of what seem to be insurmountable physical or emotional impediments." When she spoke those words with enormous conviction, we had no idea that she, too, would be tested within a few short years. Blanca suffered an automobile accident in mid-life that severely injured her spinal column and kept her wheelchair bound for the rest of her life.

Blanca Irizarry demonstrated, through sheer resolve and example, the meaning of living courageously. The last time I visited Blanca she was in fragile health with a lung condition that made her breathing extremely labored. In her late eighties, with her beloved husband, Frank, and their fluffy white dog, Andrea, at her side, she reminded me of Maslow's words and her daily challenge to be "all she could be." Our precious moments together honored a friendship that began in Puerto Rico and extended over forty years. Seeing her for the last time brought a flood of memories and underscored what she had taught me by her example of living with dignity in the midst of life challenges.

Doña Blanca, as I affectionately called her, quoted Maslow succinctly:

> *"We all have capacities, talents, missions, callings. The task is, if we are willing to take it seriously, to help ourselves to be all that we are in potentiality."*

Stumbling on Resilience

Abraham Maslow was a pioneer of "positive psychology"—a familiar buzzword these days. Browse through any book store and you will find a proliferation of titles featuring the word "happiness." Scores of studies on resilience, gratitude, and even forgiveness are making their way into academic journals and popular magazines alike.

The revolutionary idea in psychology of focusing on what is <u>right</u> rather than what is <u>wrong</u> with our lives originated with Maslow more than 50 years ago. His commitment to awakening human potential never wavered even as he approached his final years and died of a heart condition in 1970. Maslow charged that psychology was primarily interested in human shortcomings, illnesses, and troubles, with too little emphasis on potential, aspirations, and meaningful pursuits.

Maslow's widely recognized hierarchy of needs, depicted in a pyramid, speaks to a universal longing for self-actualization—for becoming all we can be. The hierarchy contains five levels of human needs: physiological, safety and security, belongingness and love, esteem and self-respect as well as self-actualization. When the needs at one level are met, we move to the next level. But when basic needs are thwarted, humans often remain in a basic survival mode.

Hierarchy of Needs

Physiological Needs: The most basic, most powerful, most obvious of all needs are physical survival—food, water, air, shelter, sleep. A person who is lacking food, self-esteem and even safety will demand *food first*. Until this basic survival need is addressed, the individual will ignore other needs or push them into the background.

Safety Needs: Once the physiological needs are sufficiently met, safety needs emerge—not only for physical safety but also consistency, fairness and a certain amount of routine.

Belongingness and Love Needs: Once the physiological and safety needs are met, love, affection and belongingness needs emerge. We seek positive relations with others in order to satisfy the universal longing to be deeply understood and accepted.

Esteem Needs: Self-respect and respect from others cover a desire for confidence, competence, adequacy, achievement, independence and freedom.

Self-Actualization Needs: What we can be, we must become. This is a longing for continuous development of our potential, a pursuit of purposefulness.

Desire to Know and Understand: A characteristic of good mental health is curiosity. Maslow's clinical experiences offer cases in which previously healthy adults suffered boredom, loss of interest in life, depression and despair. He noted that the best antidote for such stagnation is total immersion into something worthy of one's efforts. In Frankl's words, this is the *Search for Meaning*. I call it a *Search for Significance*.

Aesthetic Needs: In most persons, the need to experience beauty runs very deep. Appreciating a work of art, nature, or a sunset can bring profound satisfaction. The need for beauty is almost universally present in healthy self-actualizing people.

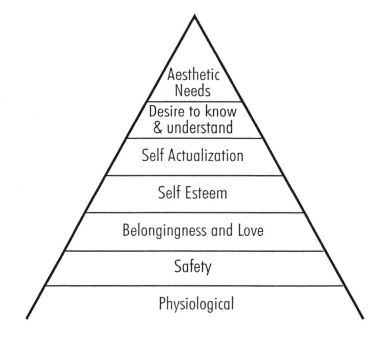

Life Review as a Pathway to Wholeness

On a rainy Seattle day in 1978, Dr. Robert Butler, Pulitzer-prize winning author of *Why Survive: Growing Old in America,* visited the University of Washington. Butler had recently taken the reins as founding director of the National Institute on Aging. At the time, I was a newly appointed faculty member with the interdisciplinary Institute on Aging and the Department of Health Education at the University. Having Robert Butler visit and share his research on Life Review was an opportunity to hear firsthand about the significance of a process that was debated in gerontological circles. And I heard a profoundly wise and compassionate man describe yet another basic human need—putting one's life in order and making sense of it in the process!

Dr. Butler reminded us that life review is a prominent developmental occurrence in later life. As early as 1961, when the field of gerontology was just emerging, Robert Butler said he recognized that many people considered reminiscing a sign of senility or living in the past. He went on to point out that the limited studies available then had been conducted on nursing home residents with chronic diseases. These studies actually tended to reinforce stereotypes of older people as confused and leading meaningless lives.

However, Dr. Butler noted that his work with patients in individual and group therapy drew him to see life review as a normal function of later years, not a pathological trait as many of his colleagues contended. In fact, Butler claimed that his patients taught him that memories, reminiscence, and nostalgia all play a part in the process of healthful aging—a vital process.

Butler told that there is a renewed capacity for free association and a sudden remarkable clarity of recaptured tastes, smells and other sensations. Some people are fully aware of the process and openly state their desire to "put my life in order." For others the trigger is a major transition or loss.

Spontaneous Life Review

A spontaneous life review event is seen especially when one is confronted by a major crisis. The intensity and emphasis placed on putting one's life in order is striking.

By reassessing past events, one may be able to come to terms with inner conflicts. This can involve reconciling with a long-estranged relative or friend, or it could simply mean forgiving oneself and or the other person and letting go of the negativity. Such reminiscence can give new significance and meaning to life and even mitigate oppressive feelings of anger, fear and anxiety.

Butler's most poignant remarks came when he reminded us to truly listen to the older person. He said: *"Health care providers who care for older persons depend far too much on drugs to quiet psychic pain. It is hard to believe that a pill has the capacity to satisfy the need to share memories with an empathic listener."*

The overall benefit of life review is that it is a vehicle to acceptance of past events. When we resolve life conflicts we are more able to be fully present in the moment. Energy is freed up for creativity.

What triggers memories? A familiar smell or sound can flood us with memories of events that happened when we were very young. Reminiscing about a happy event and savoring the memory can bring heartfelt joy.

Conversely those who have intense grief laden experiences may repress the memories until an event forces them back into awareness. An example is the terrorist attacks on New York and Washington where people who had previously lived through wartime trauma were once again confronted with sights and sounds of tragic memories.

Life review is selective; not all past experiences are remembered or shared. Recollections of historic events and the era in which they occurred are valuable eyewitness accounts of parts of a nation's heritage. Tom Brokaw's book *The Greatest Generation* shows the value of gathering the stories and experiences of those he calls "extraordinary ordinary" people. He illustrates the power of recollection and the documentation of history.

Memories are Quarries of Recollections

I believe our memories are quarries of recollections that we can mine. The process of recalling past experiences can provide a salutary opportunity for integrating the past and a linkage across generations.

Means of evoking memory and facilitating life review that I find particularly effective are described briefly.

Written or taped autobiographies: Telling our stories in written or spoken form can be a vehicle to greater self-acceptance. It is one mode of searching for significance. Sometimes when we record our thoughts and experiences, we gain greater awareness of the wisdom within.

Pilgrimages: Most of us live some distance from our origins. Sometimes we have faint recollections of sites or places of significance. A pilgrimage back to our birthplace or childhood settings can provide unexpected fulfillment.

Reunions: Related to the longing to revisit old places is the desire to "see one more time" persons with whom we grew up, went to school or worked—as well as family. Reunions provide an opportunity to reminisce and catch up on intervening events.

Genealogy: As we age, we tend to become more curious about our forebears, as if half-expecting them to form a reception committee to orient us to our place in history. Researching genealogy can be a link to ancestors and to branches of the family tree. The advent of the human genome has opened a whole new avenue to pursue our ancestors that we could not have even dreamed possible until very recently.

Memorabilia, scrapbooks, photo albums, old letters: Probably the most accessible contact with the past for most of us is through our keepsakes and written or pictorial records. Often we have stashed these away and going through them can provide gratifying hours of recollection. Once organized, our scrapbooks and mementos offer a focus for conversation with family and friends.

Summation of life work: Reflection on one's life work

is a challenging undertaking; one probably more demanding than expected. Here are some of the questions we ask ourselves: What have I done? Have I made a significant contribution? Have I been authentic?

. . Be patient towards all that is unresolved in your heart and try to love the questions themselves . . .

Rainer Maria Rilke

Story Corps

There is a remarkable project initiated by National Public Radio (NPR) that I find intriguing. It is called *Story Corps.*

The *Story Corps* recordings as heard on NPR have been inspiring people since 2003. Wherever you are, with family or with someone you just met, you can participate by telling your own stories and listening to the stories of those around you.

Listening is an Act of Love, a book that describes Story Corps says:

"Truly listening and giving your sincere attention to another can be a most therapeutic and loving activity."

David Isay, founder of *Story Corps,* encourages people everywhere to join in. To learn the locations of story booths across the USA their website is *www.storycorps.net.* There are two permanent facilities open year round in New York City where anyone interested can make an appointment and *"record your loved one's voice for history."*

If a visit to the Big Apple is not possible, Isay says: "Do it yourself. Conduct your own interview and ask the questions you've always wanted to ask. You will be surprised by the power of the experience."

Pick a storyteller: Start the process by figuring out whom you want to interview. A grandparent? An old friend? Your parents?

Be sure to remind the storyteller that you think the story is important and that it will be valuable to future generations. Let that person know you would be pleased to hear and to record his or her story. Some questions you may choose to ask are:

- What is the most important lesson you have learned in life?
- What are proud of?
- Do you have any regrets?
- What was the happiest moment of your life?
- The saddest?
- How would you like to be remembered?

Story Corps is all about giving voice to people longing to be heard; it is a valuable form of life review. Add your own questions or invite the person telling the story to add questions too. It can be a rich and fulfilling reciprocal experience.

Boom: Voices of the Sixties

Reflections on the '60s and today followed on the heels of Tom Brokaw's book about the World War II generation—that of his parents.

I awoke one morning some months ago to hear Tom Brokaw interviewed on NPR in Seattle where he was scheduled to speak that evening and hold a book signing for *Boom,* his latest book. I was struck by his comments about the period from 1963 to 1974 as "the '60s." He justified that definition by saying "history rarely cuts neatly by numbers." Then he went on to tell the interviewer that we moved swiftly from grey flannel suits of the '50s to the turbulence of the '60s. He described the assassination of President Kennedy in 1963 as the beginning of our loss of innocence.

I grabbed the pencil and pad next to my bed and jotted down the title of Brokaw's book. Later that very morning I went out and purchased *Boom.*

Who could deny that the assassination of Kennedy had impacted us forever? It was the beginning of a loss of innocence that we could not fathom. Who alive then cannot remember vividly where they were when the news broke?

I was walking slowly through the tree-lined colonial town plaza returning to the four-generation household where I lived as a Peace Corps Volunteer. I heard the news over a loudspeaker in the town square: "El Presidente de los Estados Unidos fue matado esta tarde en Dallas Texas." (The President of the United States of America was killed this afternoon in Dallas, Texas.) My ears could hear the words blurted out over the microphones but my mind could not comprehend them.

President Kennedy killed? This could not be. I was part of the Peace Corps that President Kennedy had invited us to join just the year before. This could not be true.

I walked the two blocks to the place I called home on Calle Audiencia. I entered my room just to the right of the fountain in the courtyard and collapsed on the day bed. I was dazed. Finally as I slowly removed my shoes, I looked up and saw Señora Elena, the owner of the house, weeping in the courtyard just outside my window. She had heard it too. She asked me to sit with her by the radio in her room as the news was broadcast over and over. She held my hand in hers.

Then the townspeople began coming to the door to express their condolences. You see, Kennedy was revered in Sucre. The townspeople saw Peace Corps as Kennedy's volunteers. They mourned with us. Masses were said in the churches, people dressed in black, and for several days only somber music was played over the loudspeakers in the plaza. There was no television in Bolivia in 1963, so we relied solely on the radio as the events unfolded. I had never seen such an outpouring of shock and grief anywhere. We were numbed by disbelief.

In Brokaw's book, I was especially interested to read what he had to say about those three years leading up to Kennedy's death and particularly about the Peace Corps that was such a pivotal life experience for me. I was dismayed that Tom Brokaw skipped over those early days of the '60s when I and hundreds of other young people responded to Kennedy's call:

"Ask not what your country can do for you but rather ask what you can do for your country."

This was a formative time in my life and those years as a Peace Corps Volunteer and later as a Peace Corps staff member opened pathways that I had not dreamed possible. How could anyone leave this out of a book on the '60s? And why did Brokaw only mention Peace Corps in one paragraph of one page? I realized from my reaction that I was personally immersed in my own life review.

Life review is a huge part of our *Search for Significance*. What is it all about? What am I here for? Have you engaged in life review? Have you ever thought of listening as an act of love? What are the pivotal events of your life? Would you consider recording them? What would top your list? What events have you heard friends and relatives repeat often?

An event in recent times that nearly all can remember with clarity is: "Where were you when you heard about 9/11?" Most of us can recall precisely the emotions of that moment. For my parents, the news of the bombing of Pearl Harbor was an event seared in their memories. For me, nothing has come close to the intensity of emotion I experienced when I learned of the death of President Kennedy.

I was born in the same year as Tom Brokaw—1940—also in Middle America as the horrors of World War II were occurring. I have been impacted by the Ken Burns documentary *The War*. Of the four towns in the United States that Burns chose to feature, he picked Luverne, Minnesota, my birthplace. And I remember well the stories my parents told of that day in 1941—Dec. 7—the attack on Pearl Harbor.

My parents, Aunt Janet, and Uncle John, who was home on leave from the Army, had been playing a card game of pinochle as I toddled around the dining room. The radio playing softly probably to distract me while they went on with their card game. Suddenly the radio program was interrupted with the announcement that Pearl Harbor had been attacked by Japan. My parents described Uncle John's handsome ruddy face going bloodless as he heard the news, knowing that he would be called back to duty immediately.

It wasn't until 54 years after that infamous day that I would hear directly from Aunt Janet what the announcement of the attack on Pearl Harbor meant to her and Uncle John. As I sat at her side around the clock in her California home while hospice nurses attended in her final days, I realized that listening was the most loving thing I could do for her.

Aunt Janet recalled those early days in Luverne, Minnesota, her husband's career path, and its impact on her family. She spoke of her emotions—the confusing mixture of pride, fear, anger, and loneliness she felt when John was sent on missions and she stayed behind with the two children. She spoke of the resentments and the responsibilities she shouldered when she was left to care for her elderly parents—my grandparents.

Aunt Janet spoke with deep regret about having not achieved some of her goals–especially for advanced education. But she also spoke with pride about her civic accomplishments, which included Presidential citations and numerous awards and honors for her community development work. She told me about some honors Uncle John had received that she only found among his papers after his death a few years earlier. Then the floodgates opened as she spoke of all the missed opportunities for communication. He was gone and she could not ask him about so many things.

A line from a song I had heard called *The Living Years* came to mind as I sat quietly listening to my aunt: "It's too late when we die to admit we don't see eye-to-eye. Wish I could have told him in the Living Years."

When I look back on Aunt Janet's final days, I think of Mitch Albom's book *Tuesdays with Morrie* written about a series of visits with his dying mentor and friend. Mitch recorded this about forgiveness:

"It's not just other people we need to forgive, Mitch," Morrie whispered. *"We also need to forgive ourselves."*

"Ourselves?" questioned Mitch.

"Yes," said his mentor. *"For all the things we didn't do. All the things we should have done. You can't get stuck on the regrets of what should have happened. That doesn't help you when you get to where I am."*

We all need to tell our story and to understand our story . . . We need for life to signify, to touch the eternal, to understand the mysterious and to find out who we are.

Joseph Campbell

. . . Listening is more than just not interrupting. It is acknowledging through one's active attention that the other person is being heard. Perhaps most important is that people who are sharing their feelings be assured they will not be criticized for having such feelings.

Riane Eisler

CHAPTER FIVE

Gateway to Wholeness:
Weaving the Threads
of Connection

Humankind has not woven the web of life.
We are but one thread within it.
Whatever we do to the web,
we do to ourselves.
All things are bound together.
All things connect.

Chief Seattle

Because of the interconnectedness of all
minds, affirming a positive vision may be
about the most sophisticated action any one
of us can take.

William Harman

Never doubt that a small group of thoughtful,
committed people can change the world. Indeed
it is the only thing that ever has.

Margaret Mead

A Message from the Hopi Elders

A timely message from the Hopi Elders was read and discussed in one of my seminars by LouVina Majo, a very wise and kind woman who lives between the worlds of her Hopi Nation in Arizona and Prescott, where she counsels and teaches about Native American traditions. LouVina shared valuable insights into the spiritual nature of Hopi culture and their ancient lifeways as expressed in a complex interweaving of ceremony, stories, songs, art, and agriculture. She underscored the importance of sharing stories for generations to come.

When LouVina read the message from her Elders, the seminar participants were visibly moved by its potential in their *Search for Significance.*

You have been telling the people that this is the eleventh hour
Now you must go back and tell the people that this is The Hour.
Here are the things that must be considered:
Where are you living?
What are you doing?
What are your relationships?
Are you in right relation?
Where is your water?
Know your garden.
It is time to speak your Truth.
Create your community.
Be good to each other
And do not look outside yourself for the leader.
This could be a good time!
There is a river flowing now very fast.

It is so great and swift that there are those
who will be afraid.
They will try to hold on to the shore.
They will feel like they are
being torn apart,
and they will suffer greatly.
Know the river has its destination.
The elders say we must let go of the shore,
push off toward the middle of the river.
Keep our eyes open,
and our heads above the water.
See who is there with you and celebrate.
At this time in history, we are to take nothing
personally, least of all ourselves!
For the moment we do,
our spiritual growth
and journey comes to a halt.
The time of the lone wolf is over.
Gather yourselves!
Banish the word struggle
from your attitude and vocabulary.
All that we do now must be done
in a sacred manner and in celebration.
We are the ones we have been waiting for.

> *The impossible is possible when people align with you. When you do things with people, not against them, the amazing resources of the Higher Self within are mobilized.*
>
> Gita Bellin

We are All Travelers

On a stopover in Washington, DC, enroute to Kenya and Uganda years ago, I was stunned by a message left on the pillow of an inn I checked into late one night.

I have carried this message with me for many years now. It says:

> *To our Guest:*
>
> *In ancient times there was a prayer for "The Stranger within Our Gates." Because this hotel is a human institution to serve people, and not solely a money-making organization, we hope that you will be granted peace and rest while you are under our roof.*
>
> *May this room and hotel be your "second" home. May those you love be near you in thoughts and dreams. Even though we may not get to know you, we hope that you will be comfortable and happy as if you were in you own house.*
>
> *May the business that brought you our way prosper. May every call you make and every message you receive add to your joy. When you leave, may your journey be safe.*
>
> *We are all travelers. From "birth 'til death" we travel between eternities. May these days be pleasant for you,*

*profitable for society, helpful for those
you meet, and a joy to those who know
and love you best.*

Yes, I found that message in the heart of our nation's capital! I was deeply moved by its significance
as I attended meetings with the Agency for International Development in preparation for my travels to
Kenya and Uganda. I was scheduled for an international health consulting assignment in these East African countries in the summer of 1987. By then I had
been engaged in global health work for over two decades, yet each time I traveled to a new land and a
new assignment, I was keenly aware that it was I
who was different—yet so alike everyone I would
meet. Yes, as that message on my pillow said: "we are
all travelers, just traveling between eternities."

I carry that poignant message wherever I go.
Since that day my work has taken me to Central and
South America as well as the Caribbean, Australia,
New Zealand, Indonesia, Thailand, Japan, Macedonia, East Africa and Southern Africa. All along the
way, I continue to see how our lives are all interconnected. All of us with dreams and hopes, and, yes, all
seeking meaning and purpose regardless of circumstances.

While going through notes and trip reports recently, I found my journal from a meeting with a
group of healthcare providers in Mombassa, Kenya
dated August 27, 1987. I wrote that the health division supervisors had completed a training needs assessment and were now preparing an in-service

training plan for all workers in the community health education program. My notes said "good needs assessment; organizing meeting for all directors next week to analyze results and develop an implementation strategy for training." All this was a standard part of my work assignment. I loved it.

When I looked at a loose leaf of paper tucked into the back cover of my journal, I was surprised to find some notes I had jotted down to myself that same August day. My note said:

> "Home is where your heart is . . . Be at home (here) now. Move with assurance. Live with Faith. Awaken with a song in your heart. Connect with Nature. Remember your Family extends to the World Community. Love conquers all. May you always feel its warmth and protection directly from Source."

> *"We are caught in an inescapable net-*
> *work of mutuality, tied in a single gar-*
> *ment of destiny."*
>   Martin Luther King, Jr.

Stone Soup and Open Doors

I often remember a tale that I heard from my grandmother in rural Minnesota. It is the Stone Soup
Story, which, in fact, reflected her "open door"
to strangers in our midst.

The Stone Soup story has its roots in ancient folk-
lore. Versions of the story have been traced to all
parts of the globe. Many of us remember this story
being read to us in childhood. Do you remember
hearing it? How was the story told to you? By whom?

What I recall from Grandma Annie's version of
the story is that a stranger comes into town, riding
the rails on a box car. He is hungry and alone. He
knocks on several doors and no one opens their door.
The people of the town have grown afraid of the
"tramps" or "hobos" as they refer to the transients
who hop trains. The townspeople are suspicious and
hardened to the needs of others, even their
neighbors.

The stranger gathers some twigs and branches
and begins to make a fire. He places a small tin pot
on top and fills it with water from the town well.

Then a little girl named Emily Ann, who has been
watching him asks shyly, "Sir, what are you making?"

"I am making stone soup and I need three

stones," says the stranger. Emily Ann promptly goes to find three pebbles and places them in the pot. The stranger thanks her and says, "these stones will make good soup but this small pot won't hold much soup."

Emily Ann responds quickly by running across the schoolyard to her own home and asking her mom for a large pot, one large enough for stone soup.

Emily Ann's mother is caught by surprise and intrigued as she has never heard of stone soup. Curious about Emily Ann's plea, her mother finds a large pot in the kitchen cupboard and follows her daughter out to see what this stranger's request was all about.

As smoke from the fire drifts up, one by one the people begin peering out their windows and then venturing outside to see what stone soup really is. The stranger suggests ingredients like potatoes, vegetables and seasonings to make the soup more plentiful. And then something magical begins to happen. As each person begins to give, the next person goes to find something more to add to the soup: cauliflower, rutabagas, peas, carrots, peppers, corn, potatoes, pumpkin, quinoa, Brussels sprouts, broccoli, and much more. The soup takes on a rich and delicious aroma and the pot is boiling to the ready.

The people gather together to taste the soup. They have not been together for a feast like this for as long as anyone can remember. They tell stories well into the evening and then several offer the stranger a place to sleep.

The next morning the townspeople gather to say goodbye to the stranger. He thanks them and they in turn say to him: "You have opened our hearts."

Now, in today's world, you might say, "that guy is a con artist." Or "that could not happen in our town." Or "why on earth did Emily Ann's mother not warn her about talking to strangers?" "What kind of mother is that?"

What would be the reaction in your neighborhood if such a stranger showed up?

If our goal is to create a beloved community, this will require a qualitative change in our souls as well as a quantitative change in our lives.

Martin Luther King, Jr.

In Prescott, Arizona, where I live and work part of the year, there is a community outreach program called Open Door, which resides in the basement of a downtown sanctuary. I think Open Door is living the stone soup legacy. In fact, at Open Door soup is standard fare offered to those who stop by for support. They are also offered clothing, counseling and emergency housing for families in need. The beauty of it is that sometimes those same strangers whom Open Door has served come back to volunteer their help. Some bring a bag of clothing or an extra loaf of bread or a can of vegetables to share as an expression of gratitude.

What goes around comes around,
this I've learned with Time.
What you give you always get back.
What you sow,
you reap in kind.
Always be helpful to others
and give what you can spare
for being kind to strangers,
we may help Angels unaware.

Anonymous

The Web of the World

In 1991, as I was giving a series of seminars in Australia on Life Review and Logotherapy, I was discussing the work of Viktor Frankl and its relevance for people of all ages. As has been my experience everywhere I speak, people resonated deeply with Frankl's three pronged message for finding meaning: **doing a deed, loving, and even suffering.**

Health and social service providers attending that seminar in Sydney were relating their stories and experiences to the group when a young man spoke up. "Dr. Marr Burdman, in this audience is our own Marjorie Pizer, a world-renowned poet who has lots to say about meaning and interconnectedness." Others nodded in recognition as he motioned toward the front of the room.

I invited Marjorie Pizer, a stately yet unassuming

middle-aged woman seated in the second row, to share a poem with us. She graciously accepted and rose to speak. Her poem "Web of the World" touched us deeply.

In her clear, confident, and resonant voice Marjorie recited:

"In the whole web woven of the being of the world
Each of us has a place,
A small corner of the tapestry uniquely ours,
Spun in with our times and those around us.
We weave our own corner into its own shape
And the tiny shapes become the whole,
And the whole moulds the little shapes
Until all are become part of one another.
No matter how small, all are required;
Each touches the whole and becomes a part of it.
Even you, even a small lizard touches and changes
The skirts of the universe."

Alliance for a New Humanity

At a gathering in Puerto Rico in 2002, the Argentinean writer Ernesto Sábato, then in his ninth decade, invited participants "to come together to recover, to create a new narrative that includes all of us in a family of humanity. . . to give space again, in the soul of the people, to an utopia that encompasses values like love for the human being, justice, a sense of honor, honesty, respect for others and the search for the sacred meaning of life."

These words of Ernesto Sábato were the seeds from which an Alliance for a New Humanity took root. The Alliance was formed to bring forth a sustainable, equitable and peaceful world.

Deepak Chopra, Oscar Arias, Arsenio Rodriguez and many others are spearheading this global movement. All are invited to participate.

At the 2005 Alliance for a New Humanity Forum in Puerto Rico, I was profoundly impacted by the passion and commitment to the call to raise a global vision of higher understanding and interconnection. The conference weaver, Duncan Campbell, reminded us that from time immemorial, beginning with indigenous councils and ancient wisdom traditions and through the work of physicist David Bohm, and others, mutually participatory dialogue has been seen as the key to evolving and transforming consciousness. Evoking a flow of meaning takes us well beyond what one individual can bring through alone. Once again I remembered Viktor Frankl's advice to me years before:

"Listen to the person on the street. He or
she will be your teacher."

Who is that person on your street? In the market? On the subway? Or seated with you at the conference table? Or anywhere you find yourself?

Are we listening? What are we hearing? If we can stay awake when our lives are changing, secrets will be revealed to us about ourselves, about the nature of life, and about the eternal source of meaning that is always available and that is renewable day by day.

Duncan Campbell calls this awakening "a fire-keeping space where together we can ignite each other's unique creative spark to bring forth our individual transformation and the evolution of our global community."

Listen to the Voice Within

Voices of other contemporary visionaries are calling us again and again, "Wake up, wake up!"

James O'Dea, President of the Institute of Noetic Sciences says:

> *"When we understand that the core impulse of every religion is good and noble, we find our way to unity and peace. When we understand the interdependence of all life on Earth, we thrive in the context of creative collaboration with each other and with Nature. When we understand the potential within each human being, we will wake up to the importance of developing the inner life. In every age, mystics, sages, and teachers have shown us how to go deep within and, by doing do, experience the great gift of awareness itself. Listen to the voice within."*

In a recent letter to friends of the Alliance for a New Humanity, Deepak Chopra writes: "the seeds are germinating. Our joint efforts are bearing the first fruits. Now we need to scale up our energies, our connectivity, our love, to generate an ever increasing wave of transformation. Imagine, celebrate, co-create, commit yourself to the change and to make a difference. Come share your vision for a better world."

The breeze at dawn has secrets to tell you.
Don't go back to sleep.
You must ask for what you really want.
Don't go back to sleep.
People are going back and forth across the
doorsill
Where the two worlds touch.
The door is round and open.
Don't go back to sleep.
Rumi

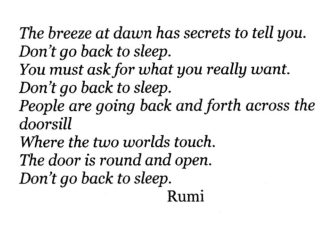

CHAPTER SIX

Self and Soul:
Standing Tall with Deep Roots

Everybody needs beauty . . . Places to play and pray in, where Nature may heal and cheer and give strength to body and soul alike.

John Muir

There is one spectacle grander than the sea, That is the sky; There is one spectacle grander than the sky, That is the interior of the soul.

Victor Hugo

The morning glory which blooms for an hour differs not at the heart from the giant pine Which lives for a thousand years.

Zen poem

Walking the World in a Sacred Way was the theme of a conference that I participated in a few years ago among the ancient red rocks of Sedona, Arizona. I heard a call from the anthropologist, Angeles Arrien, as she bid us to:

**"Stand tall . . . with deep roots
and know who you are!"**

That invitation from Basque anthropologist, teacher, and pathfinder Arrien resonated with me and was a reminder of a quote by Albert Einstein that I had read on a park bench plaque years earlier:

**"Look deep into nature, and there
you will understand everything
better."**

I see the miraculous renewing capacity of the tree, ever changing with the seasons, as a metaphor for the process of human life in its continuous growth and unfoldment. Especially, the symbolism of the evergreen tree with its stately branches is life itself deeply rooted and connected to its Source.

Trees are at once a symbol of growth, renewal, and transformation. In Eugene, Oregon, a place I call my "Heart Home," I was fortunate to live in a thickly forested area in the 1970s when I taught gerontology and community health education courses at the University of Oregon. Each morning a local radio station played the popular John Denver piece *Annie's Song*:
"You wake up my senses like a night in the forest."
The song was a magnificent reminder to awaken to a new day with all its challenges and

opportunities for growth. I loved it.

My memories of a gnarled old oak tree and the white-tailed deer that came to lick a salt block we had placed at the foot of that particular tree are as vivid now as they were several decades ago. Why?

Trees have personal emotional significance for me and for many people I meet along my path. In fact, I find that most people have vivid feelings and associations connected with trees. In my workshops and seminars, I frequently invite participants to remember a tree that was significant in years past. Then we share stories. "Once upon a time . . . "

The stored memories that come pouring fourth are breathtaking. At a workshop in Seattle, Angela, a thirty-five-year old mother of three shared a remembrance of apple trees from her early childhood. Angela's single working mother borrowed a friend's car for a day and took her to visit an orchard in Central Washington. Angela recalled that after reveling in a glorious autumn afternoon of picking a bucket full of red gala apples, her mother reminded her "these apples are to share with our neighbors." She said simply "The abundance that is ours today must be shared."

Angela went on to tell how she strives to impart that lesson to her own children. She shared the profound significance of her mother's example of living with an abundant heart in spite of limited resources.

Mark, a forty-year old outdoor enthusiast, remembered his annual family jaunt by car from Seattle to Los Angeles to visit his grandparents when he was in elementary school. He recalled his "total awe" as they passed through the Giant Sequoia trees in Northern California. He could hardly wait each year to ride through the forest, home to the most massive trees on this planet.

Mark is now an avid proponent of the Sierra Club and noted with sadness that over half of the remaining Sequoia groves are at risk. He asked us to join in the effort to protect Sequoia National Monument. He said, "we need to work for protection for these majestic trees—these living monuments." With a quivering voice, Mark went on to say that "without permanent protection, even trees that take centuries to grow are at risk."

Trees do evoke strength and protection. I think Mark is among those people who have such vivid emotional recollections of trees that the idea of communicating with them seems quite natural.

Viktor Frankl was fond of relating a story of his encounter with a terminally ill girl who knew she was dying. Asked how she could be so cheerful even though her time was short, his young patient pointed to a small tree just outside her window. She said of the tree: **"I am able to talk with the tree; it is a friend."** Frankl asked if the tree replied to her. She answered: **"Yes, it says: I am here, I am here, I am Life."**

Standing Tall With Deep Roots

Viktor Frankl, though slight in physical stature, stood tall. His exhortation **"Listen to the person on the street; he or she will be your teacher!"** came to me clearly just a few days ago as I stopped by the extensive and ever-expanding—and expensive—Bellevue Square shopping center in Bellevue, Washington, just east of Seattle.

Bellevue is a rapidly growing and affluent community. Bell Square (as it is called by locals) is just a couple of miles from Bill and Melinda Gates' neighborhood. I point to this geographical fact because this remarkable couple, through the Gates Foundation, has a commitment to global health and well-being for all humans that is unrivaled in its philanthropic mission. In the United States, their work seeks to ensure that all people—especially those with the fewest resources—have access to opportunities they need to succeed in school and life. The Gates' vision and work is about *Generativity* and *Living Your Legacy* that I discuss in the next chapter.

Communities of Complex Lives

In Bellevue, however, there is another less visible community just two miles to the east of Bell Square— a community of relatively recent immigrants from all parts of the globe. These families with complex and challenging lives have caught the attention of the affluent.

Tucked into a corner of the elegant Bell Square is the Overlake Service League Thrift Shop. A cadre of volunteers maintains a space filled with used clothing, toys, books and sundry other items donated by area residents as they enter the mall to "shop" the Nordstroms, Tiffany, Eddie Bauer, Ann Taylor, and other upscale stores.

I like to drop by the thrift shop because there are

incredible bargains to be had—some slightly worn and some never worn garments from the likes of Eileen Fisher, Dana Buchman, and other "names"—you get the picture.

I wondered why such beautiful clothing that had hardly been worn would be donated so regularly. That is, until I began to hear counseling clients tell me that sometimes while desperately looking for a semblance of purpose in their lives, they spend their days shopping. Some even say they gather up their newly purchased clothing and drop it off at the thrift shop as they enter the mall to go shopping—just to fill their day. And there are even those who call it "retail therapy!" I see this as a desperate cry for meaning, an unheard cry for significance. And that cry often comes from the affluent in our communities. The *Search for Significance* has many faces.

Quiet Grace

Often the humblest among us are the great teachers. All we need to do is stop and listen. The other day as I was looking around the thrift shop, a tall East African woman with a tiny babe in arms walked up to me and held a fuchsia colored raw silk dress to her ebony face and asked my advice: "Do you think this suits me? Would I dare wear it?"

I answered: "Of course, it is beautiful!" I commented that her baby was precious and she smiled and went about looking through the racks of children's clothing.

Then I overheard this humble yet regal African woman quietly speak to a child in the yellow alcove filled with used toys: "Now place them all back on the shelves," she said gently.

I looked into the toy-lined niche and saw a bright eyed boy about three years old playing with a John Deere tractor on the floor. I said, "Oh, you have another child."

She smiled at me and said "two more," just as a kindergarten-age girl with pink ribbons in her tightly braided hair peeked up from the Disney puzzle she was piecing together.

I commented, "Your children are so well-mannered and you are very patient and kind."

She looked at me with a gracious and elegant smile and simply said: *"I love them so."* The mother-child bond and the presence of Spirit was palpable.

As this Mother paid for her few articles of clothing with coupons from the Service League and left the store with her three children in hand, I realized that I had encountered a teacher—the kind of teacher that Frankl reminded us to look for and listen to!

That Mother touched my life with her Quiet Grace. I saw a Teacher in our midst "Standing Tall and Shining Light." That brief moment at the thrift shop goes into my treasured memory bank.

This I Believe

As I reflect on my personal journey, I am convinced that our memories are quarries we can mine at will. I believe that examining of our experiences is really about finding our voice and knowing what we stand for . . . indeed, **stand tall** for!

I always perk up when I hear *This I Believe* essays read on National Public Radio. Initiated by Jay Allison and Dan Gediman, the program consists of essays about the personal philosophies of men and women—some well-known and others not known at all. And now they have a book of selected essays by the same title: *This I Believe, The Personal Philosophies of Remarkable Men and Women*. In his introduction, Jay Allison says simply:

> " *This I Believe* offers a simple if difficult invitation. Write a few hundred words expressing the core principles that guide your life—your personal credo. "

The invitation is issued to anyone—politicians, nurses, artists, construction workers, athletes, parents, students, and others. Writers of selected essays are invited to read them on public radio to an audience of millions.

This I Believe was first broadcast in 1951 with Edward R. Morrow hosting. Fifty years after the original series ended, Allison and Gediman decided it was time to bring it back to radio.

Allison and Gediman note that matters of belief divide our country and our world today much as they did when the series was first broadcast. We find ourselves in the midst of change and challenge over healthcare, economics, politics and issues of ethnicity and faith. Yet there seems to be little time for deep and compassionate listening to the views of others.

For *This I Believe* essayists, including you and me and anyone who cares to participate, the rules are simple:

Frame your beliefs in positive terms. Refrain from dwelling on what you do not believe. Focus on your story, be brief, name your belief, be positive, be personal. And all this in one hundred words!

Have you thought of framing your beliefs in a story? What pops into your mind when you think of your core belief? Where was it formed? How was it formed? Can you find expression for it?

You Only Have What you Give

Of all the stories that have piqued my interest in the NPR series, it is the Isabel Allende essay that I keep revisiting. Yes, the diminutive, fiery, Chilean author Isabel Allende stopped to write and speak her *This I Believe* after her beloved twenty-eight-year old daughter, Paula, died in her arms in 1992.

Isabel Allende said that during that first year of deep grief everything stopped for her:

"However, that year also gave me an opportunity to reflect upon my journey and the principles that hold me together. I discovered that there is consistency in my beliefs, my writing, and the way I lead my life. Paula taught

*me a lesson that is now my man-
tra: You only have what you give. It's
by spending yourself that you become
rich."*

Standing Tall With No Fear

Another lesson that I continue to revisit is a quote
from Nelson Mandela's 1994 inaugural address in
South Africa when he spoke these words attributed
to Marianne Williamson:

*"Our deepest fear is not that we are
inadequate. Our deepest fear is that
we are powerful beyond measure. It is
our light, not our darkness that fright-
ens us . . . It is not just in some of us; it
is in everyone. And, as we let our own
light shine, we unconsciously give
other people permission to do the
same. As we are liberated from our
own fear, our presence automatically
liberates others."*

A few years after Nelson Mandela was elected
President of South Africa, the American Public
Health Association, an organization where I have
been a member for over thirty years, presented him
with an award. In his acceptance speech, Nelson
Mandela said he was deeply honored "because it
comes from those who are dedicated to the public
health and wellbeing of their nation, an organization
that also cares for the health of people across the
world. Your support was essential to our victory,
which is also your victory."

I heard an interview on NPR with one of my favorite writers, Maya Angelou, on her 80th birthday. She said in that deep, wise voice "Things are better now, but not as good as when you put your shoulder to the wheel."

Then I looked up at a wallhanging in my bedroom with Maya Angelou's words emblazoned on it:

> *I believe in living a poetic life, an art full life. Everything we do, from the way we raise our children to the way we welcome our friends, is part of a large canvas we are creating.*

Nelson Mandela and Maya Angelou stand tall with deep roots.

CHAPTER SEVEN

Generativity:
Living Your Legacy

. . . Peace that passes understanding can reached only by compassion. This is the ideal that must illumine, from the very center, all our efforts to bring a better life to our world, within our own country, and in the farthest reaches of the planet.

R. Sargent Shriver

"He changed my life," Bill Moyers said at a reunion in Washington, D.C. honoring Sargent Shriver, the founding Director of Peace Corps. Moyers, the broadcast journalist and author, famous for his eloquent and incisive interviews on public television was also the Deputy Director of Peace Corps at its inception. Now many of my Peace Corps friends consider him a voice for the "Conscience of America." Bill Moyers gets to the heart of humanity, and his decency and unrelenting passion for truth are his legacy too.

Moyers' career as a television journalist has earned him multiple honors over the years. His reporting and interviews have been the basis for bestselling books including *The Power of Myth, Listening to America, Healing and the Mind, The Language of Life*, and *Genesis*.

Now after his "retirement," he is back on public television every Friday night with *Bill Moyers Journal*. It is one of the highlights of my week. Those who say television is a vast wasteland have not been watching PBS on Friday nights! Bill Moyers and his guests push me to think deeply about what really matters in this life.

In his tribute to Sargent Shriver, Moyers reeled off movements that Shriver and his wife Eunice Kennedy Shriver inspired: Peace Corps, Head Start, VISTA, Job Corps, Community Action, Upward Bound, Foster Grandparents, Special Olympics. At that Peace Corps reunion in D.C., Bill Moyers reminded us that Shriver lived his life with the certainty that what we do to serve, help and care for our fellow human beings is what counts in the long run.

I could also say that Sargent Shriver changed my life. My Peace Corps experience in Bolivia continues to have a profound impact on my journey to this day. I am still in regular contact now by phone and e-mail with my Bolivian friends and "family," and have returned to Sucre several times over the past four decades. Among my extended family there is a little girl named Pilar Geri, the granddaughter of one of my dearest friends, Paulina Porcel de Cervantes. My Bolivian friends have gifted and blessed me with their generous spirit and loyal friendship in innumerable ways, and gratitude is forever embedded in my heart.

Senator Hubert Humphrey of Minnesota, an early proponent of Peace Corps, also influenced the course of my life. I remember Humphrey from my high school years in rural Minnesota, when I met him at a banquet in St. Paul, the State Capital, where he honored the final contestants of a statewide radio speaking contest.

My radio address was titled: *We Build Walls.* As I write this, I am looking at my original typewritten radio speech that took me to that state contest. I found it among my mother's papers. Now I look back with considerable awe at Mother's nurturance of my passion for global work.

The radio speech that I wrote in 1958—just fifty years ago—began:

> *"Wherever we turn today we find that America is building more walls than ever before. Some walls are designed to provide shelter and privacy, some to support rafters and a roof; some walls are designed to keep people out, and others, such as those of prisons, are designed to keep people in. The one thing they have in common is that sooner or later, many of them will*

come tumbling down.

If man's wall-building program would stop with those he can build by hand, we could term him constructive, but man builds walls within himself, cutting him off from the rest of the world. Thus he loses a battle within himself, for these walls imprison him with even greater problems.

The walls of prejudice, the walls of misunderstanding, and the walls of selfishness will crumble only when people are willing to seek knowledge, realizing that knowledge leads to understanding, and understanding leads to good will."

Senator Humphrey's infectious enthusiasm for the potential of young people to contribute to the world community ignited my passion to "know the world." I thought my ticket out of rural Minnesota was to become a nurse and then see where it took me. People often say "timing is everything!" I graduated from nursing and became a full fledged RN in 1961, the very year Peace Corps was born.

I ventured to the city of Chicago to take my first job in a large teaching hospital and enrolled in night classes at Northwestern University—all the while dreaming that I might get to be part of President Kennedy's call to action. So I went to the courthouse and filled out the voluminous forms required to apply to Peace Corps.

The next step was to register for the written exam

that allowed me to complete the application process. I remember entering the vast and daunting Cook County courthouse where I had to report to take the exam. It was the coldest morning on record for November 1961. The icy wind off Lake Michigan sent a chill through my body that I am not likely to forget. Maybe it was fear of rejection that set my teeth chattering. I will never know.

I made it through the application process and then came several weeks of waiting. I tried to not get my hopes too high. I knew there were many others vying for positions in the new Peace Corps that President Kennedy embraced so heartily.

Then one January afternoon when I got off duty at the medical-surgical unit at Wesley Memorial Hospital, I walked briskly back to the nurses residence. It was still cold! As I entered the stately brick building and passed by the front desk, the receptionist called out: "Miss Marr, you have a telegram." I had never before received a telegram. So you can imagine my excitement when I opened that Western Union envelope and read the telegram from Sargent Shriver inviting me to train for the first Public Health group to go to Bolivia. I was ecstatic. Yes, my mother kept that telegram too! It read:

GERALDENE MARR
201 EAST DELAWARE PL. CHGO.
I AM HAPPY TO INFORM YOU THAT YOU HAVE BEEN SELECTED TO ENTER TRAINING FOR A PEACE CORPS BOLIVIA PROJECT. FURTHER INFORMATION WILL BE MAILED TO YOU TODAY. I AM SENDING YOU THIS TELEGRAM SO THAT IF

YOU ARE AVAILABLE YOU MAY BEGIN RE-
ARRANGING YOUR PERSONAL PLANS. PLEASE
WIRE COLLECT REGARDING YOUR AVAILABIL-
ITY AS SOON AS YOU HAVE RECEIVED ADDI-
TIONAL MATERIALS, ATTN: BOLIVIA PROJECT,
SELECTION DIVISION, PEACE CORPS, WASH-
INGTON 25,D.C.
ROBERT SARGENT SHRIVER, JR.

I went immediately to an atlas to find out where
in the world this country Bolivia was located. I knew
virtually nothing about Bolivia or Bolivians. I quickly
gleaned that Bolivia is a landlocked country in the
heart of South America, home to Aymara, Quechua
and Guarani indigenous people. La Paz is the highest
capital in the world at 11,800 feet and Sucre, the
original capital, is located in the temperate semi-
mountainous region.

A few days later when I received the packet of
materials that Sargent Shriver had promised in his
telegram, I learned that I was among the first few
hundred Peace Corps Volunteers selected to serve in
the early days of 1962. Shriver was a charismatic and
idealistic leader and we volunteers knew we were
part of a positive and significant movement. It was a
time of great hope. President Kennedy's call became
our mantra:

> **"Ask not what your country can
> do for you. Ask what you can do
> for your country."**

To this day, I regard the Peace Corps experience
as the pivotal event in my life and my awakening to a

global consciousness. In his book, *Counselor*, Ted Sorenson writes, **"The Peace Corps was one of John F. Kennedy's proudest achievements, the epitome of his call for service and sacrifice, and an important new instrument to communicate to other countries the best of American values."**

Sargent Shriver reminded us as we departed for our countries of service that in essence, all of us are members of the same great human endeavor and that our tents are merely pitched on different grounds. Shriver cautioned us to "go abroad aware that the only change that really matters must come from within." And, he told us, "you need to realize the world is home to all." Furthermore, he said "you are to bring the world back home to share what you learned with our fellow citizens." Quite an assignment for a 22-year old.

Remembering the Legacy of an Era

As I write this, Caroline Kennedy has celebrated her 50th birthday and was featured on the cover of AARP magazine. And Maria Shriver authored another significant book about living authentically— *Just Who Will You Be?* Maria pledges:

> *"I will try to help my aging parents deal with infirmity and live with dignity because that gives me peace."* She says: *"I will continue to pass along my life's lessons, because that gives me joy. Remember: You are the only per-*

son on this planet with your story. What's the point of being here unless you share it, pass it on, and help somebody else?"

What a reminder of the passage of time. An invitation to ponder the legacy of an era! These examples of generativity bring to mind others who demonstrate their deep concern for future generations. Caring about younger people is a hallmark of *generativity*, a term coined by Erik and Joan Erikson, who defined generativity as a concern for establishing and guiding the next generation. Our legacy lies within the demonstration of our core values, our truths and our love for others. It is really our commitment to do unto others . . .

Generativity in Action

A recent article in the Seattle Times newspaper talked about civic activist Kay Bullitt, who at 80 has worked long and hard for peace, social justice, historic preservation and international understanding. "Also she puts on a great picnic," the article stated. It seems that every Wednesday evening in July for the past 47 years, Kay has invited family, neighbors, and friends to spread their blankets and baguettes at her Capitol Hill home.

I became aware of this amazing woman's depth and breadth of concern for humankind when I was invited to Kay's home in the early 1990s for a gathering of women of all ages and backgrounds to dialogue about the evolving global movement then called Women of Vision.

Kay Bullitt and her gatherings and picnics lead to connectivity. Her home, a welcoming open space elegant in its simplicity, charmed me with its high ceilings and windows overlooking bountiful Northwest ferns and rhododendrons. For decades she offered her home to be a catalyst for community service.

I learned that Kay Bullitt's picnics began when her five children were young. She decided to start a tradition so her kids would be comfortable inviting their friends into their home. Now people from all parts of the globe attend the picnics. People bring their own food, and Kay provides melon, ice cream bars, and coffee.

When asked "If food isn't the main ingredient, what is the secret?" Kay simply says, "It isn't formal. You know, it is really something anyone can do. If you don't have a big yard, gather friends and go to a park. Start your tradition." She adds, "the picnics reinforce whatever good things people are doing in their lives. They find other people with similar interests and they're encouraged to connect."

Kay has held hundreds of intergenerational activities right in her back yard. One can only guess at how many lives her generous spirit has affected. It was at her home that I learned of the global movement founded by Rama Vernon, *Women of Vision and Action*. A core principle of WOVA reflects generativity:

> *"Practice compassion, courage and spirit-infused action in our daily lives and in fulfilling our purpose in life."*

Living Legacies

Another whose legacy has made a significant impact in our world is Rachel Carson, author of *Silent Spring*. Her writing made a lasting contribution to the environmental movement, and when she died in 1964, she left a substantial bequest to the Sierra Club. In 2007, the Sierra Club honored and celebrated the hundredth anniversary of her birth. Born in the Allegheny valley town of Springdale, Pennsylvania, Carson's mother instilled in her a strong sense of independence and a love of nature.

Carson held an ecological view of nature. She wrote of the interconnectedness of all living things: humans, plants, animals and farms as elements in the "web of life." *Silent Spring,* written in 1962, made her one of the most important authors of our time. Her plea and her legacy resonate loudly today:

> *"It's always so easy to assume that someone else is taking care of things. Trusting so-called authority is not enough. A sense of personal responsibility is what we desperately need."*

Al Gore, recipient of the 2007 Nobel Peace Prize, stated when he visited Rachel Carson's homestead in Pennsylvania to honor the anniversary of her birth:

> *"It is really for all of our children and grandchildren and great-grandchildren that we fight to protect the air we breathe and the water we drink, and it's for them that we also fight to honor the legacy of Rachel Carson."*

Al Gore's passionate commitment to furthering this message is an extraordinary example of generativity, a concern for the children of tomorrow. In his acceptance of the Nobel Peace Prize on December 10, 2007, Gore said:

> *"The distinguished scientists with whom it is the greatest honor of my life to share this award have laid before us a choice between two different futures—a choice that to my ears echoes the words of an ancient prophet: Life or death, blessings or curses. Therefore, choose life, that both thou and thy seed may live."*

Generativity in Health Care

A vibrant living example of generativity is the work of Marie Manthey, a global nursing leader. Inspired by Margaret Wheatley, a renowned leadership and organizational development expert who encourages dialogue, Marie Manthey, after 50 years in highly visible and dynamic nursing leadership roles, holds "nursing salons" in her home in Minneapolis. The nursing salon group is guided by the love and pursuit of wisdom through dialogue.

Manthey sets the tone and facilitates each meeting. She begins with a confidentiality statement: "What people say here stays here." This enables participants to talk freely without worrying about repercussions. One nurse said, "Manthey's powerful presence draws you in."

In these days of change and challenge in nursing and health care professions, having a wise elder such as Marie Manthey steer and guide the conversations and inquiry is a gift to younger nurses. Through her words and deeds, Marie Manthey demonstrates genuine concern for the ethics of her profession. She sets an example for others to emulate.

Another nurse leader deeply committed to generativity is Dr. JoEllen Goertz Koerner. Her book *Healing Presence: The Essence of Nursing* is an invitation to a new generation of nurses to re-engage with passion and commitment. JoEllen explores ways—scientific, creative, and spiritual—of understanding the power and impact of a "healing presence" on both the caregiver and those receiving care. She says, "when there is congruence between who nurses are and what they do, nurses bring their souls to work. This balance is experienced as a healing presence that encourages the patient's self-healing capacity." JoEllen is a way-shower for future generations of health care providers.

Joy Nugent of Adelaide, Australia is a courageous palliative care nursing leader. Joy directs the Nurse-Link Foundation whose motto is: "Putting Heart and Soul into Care." In a recent e-mail Joy wrote: " . . . our government announced that there will be Medicare rebates for nurse visits. This is what I and other nurses have been striving to achieve for 20 years— nurses recognized in this country in their own right."

Joy tells me "we are working 'round the clock' to make our software and manuals available to a new generation of nurses." That is generativity in action. Bravo!

Generativity of Parents and Grandparents

The deepest desire in a parent's heart is to see our children become who they are meant to be. Children need to know they are here for a reason. There is a purpose and a catalyst for growth in every event, action, deed, and thought.

As parents and grandparents, what we teach children is really what we must continue to learn ourselves. The highest goal in life is to find one's purpose and live by it. Indeed, a life of purpose reveals the significance of life.

The words of the Lebanese poet Kahlil Gibran are a potent reminder:

Your children are not your children.
They are the sons and daughters of life's longing for itself.
They come through you but not from you,
And though they are with you
they belong not to you.
You may strive to be like them,
but seek not to make them like you.
For life goes not backward
nor tarries with yesterday.

CHAPTER EIGHT

Springboard to Wellness:
Attitudinal Healing

Come to the edge!
We can't, we're afraid.
Come to the edge!
We can't, we will fall.
Come to the edge!
And they came,
He pushed them,
And they flew.

Guilaume Apolinaire

Edges . . . oh, edges! How many times have you been invited to the edge? How often have you felt yourself on the edge of a precipice, invited or uninvited? What happens? Fear at first—of course. We are all afraid.

That poem *Come to the Edge* was read by Elisabeth Kübler-Ross as about fifty people of all walks of life–physicians, nurses, social workers, dying patients, bereaved daughters and sons and parents—stood around a bonfire one crisp autumn evening at a Franciscan retreat center near Three Rivers, California in 1977. We had just concluded an intensive week-long workshop titled: *Life, Death, and Transitions.* It was an invitation to face the fears we all have of letting go. And indeed that is what Elisabeth guided us to do.

Among that group of participants was a woman whose entire family—mother, father and brother—had died in the preceding six months. She was numb with grief and almost mute.

Also present was a mid-life couple in deep grief over the death of their 18-year old son, a high school honor student, bound for an Ivy League university. He died in a car crash after an all-night graduation party. That father's intense grief was expressed in fury, anger at his son for having gone to the party and anger at himself for allowing his only son to attend that fatal event.

There was the physician whose brother had been murdered in a drive-by shooting, furious that the police had botched the investigation.

A forty-year old single woman on hospice care with ovarian cancer had received a personal invitation from Elisabeth to attend the workshop. That valiant woman showed us an indomitable spirit—and the significance of "living one day at a time."

Rita, a mid-life widow traveled from her home in Australia after her beloved husband Jack, her soulmate, died suddenly. Bereft, she felt totally unprepared to raise their two young boys. So intense was the outpouring of community grief that Rita's neighbors collected the funds for her to make the trip. They had heard of the Swiss psychiatrist Elisabeth Kübler-Ross and thought Rita would benefit from the workshop. Indeed she did. Rita Ward shortly thereafter became the organizer for Elisabeth's work throughout Australia and is a respected advocate for palliative care throughout her country to this day.

There were other attendees grieving over losses of all kinds, death, lost love, purposelessness, meaninglessness. Many expressed feelings similar to the existential vacuum that Frankl spoke of—not knowing how to grasp the fraying fabric of their lives.

Then I learned that a hallmark of all Kübler-Ross workshops was their mix of people and experiential nature. Yes, Elisabeth wanted to reach health care providers, clergy, funeral directors and other professionals. But even more she wanted to reach out to the dying and the bereaved.

Elisabeth's primary motivation was to teach us all about letting go of fear! Indeed we learned from one another and deeply felt our common vulnerability and our common humanity. I could not have predicted the interconnectivity that would manifest from that experiential week of learning and grieving and healing.

In the most amazingly perceptive way, Elisabeth guided each of us throughout that week to peel away our layers of resistance to facing our pain and our issues—akin to peeling away layers of onion skins. She knew precisely when to allow silence and quiet compassion to do the teaching as one by one we gathered to share our stories in a safe and nurturing atmosphere among the pines of northern California.

At that time, I was teaching at the University of Oregon, eager to take back extra-curricular content for my gerontology students. Little did I know what an experiential week it would be—a week of intensive learning that no textbook could come close to.

Throughout the week, Elisabeth shared numerous examples of how we treat life's grief and pain as something to be avoided at all costs. But, she asserted, " these experiences are really gifts." Then she spoke of the "little deaths" . . . the losses that occur in all our lives—loss of physical capacities, loss of friends, jobs, security, stature, homes, and others.

What about the "gift" of pain and loss? That was a big one to swallow. But then I remembered Frankl's three ways of finding meaning: love, service, and suffering. I mentioned my commitment to integrating Frankl's philosophy and psychology into my own work. Elisabeth responded, "Yes, Geri, when any of us look back at the anguish, suffering, and traumas in our lives, we will see that these are the periods of greatest growth. After a loss that brings you intensely painful times, you are a different person. Of course," she added "you cannot tell parents who have just lost a child that they will see the event as a great growth experience."

We asked, almost collectively, "What do you say to parents after the death of a child?" Elisabeth said, "I don't give a pat answer. First you have to see what they are feeling. Can they talk about it? Are they in a state of shock? Often they are numb and cannot say or do anything. Once they put into words what they want to say, the come out of the numbness, shock and denial. Then comes great grief. But with the grief comes anger and anguish. They look for someone or something to blame, often turning the anger on themselves. They vent all kinds of anger." Then she added, "Dying children are much less afraid than grownups . . . life is full of losses, big and small."

We asked, "How is our reaction to death different from our feelings about other losses in life?"

Elisabeth reminded us that deep grief is a reaction that happens with any loss, not just death. It happens if you are separated or divorced, or if you lose a boyfriend or a girlfriend, or if you have lived in your home for 50 years and are then compelled to move to a nursing home. Many people experience intense grief when they lose a pet. Elisabeth reminded all of us that we must "live in such a way that you say those things while the other person can still hear it. What do you think dying people teach you? They teach how to live. That is all."

> *It is only when we truly know and understand that we have a limited time on earth—and that we have no way of knowing when our time is up—that we begin to live each day to the fullest, as if it were the only one we had.*
> Elisabeth Kübler-Ross

I was reminded once again to pay close attention to what events had guided me thusfar and to recognize the teachers appearing on my path. Every single encounter has a lesson if we tune in.

I invite you to read this drama, *Walk Down a Different Street*. What does it say to you? Which street are you walking on? Who or what has appeared on your street? What did you see? What did you hear?

WALK DOWN A DIFFERENT STREET
(A Drama in Five Acts---author unknown)

Act One
I walk down the street. There is a deep hole in the sidewalk. I fall in. I am lost. I am helpless. It isn't my fault. It takes forever to find a way out

Act Two
I walk down the same street. There is a deep hole in the sidewalk. I pretend I don't see it. I fall in again. I can't believe I'm in the same place, but it isn't my fault. It still takes a long time to get out.

Act Three
I walk down the same street. There is a deep hole in the sidewalk. I see it is there. I fall in. It's a habit, but my eyes are open. I know where I am. It is my fault. I get out immediately.

Act Four
I walk down the same street. There is a deep hole in the sidewalk. I walk around it.

Act Five
I walk down a different street.

Attitude is Perspective

Have you ever stopped to contemplate the magnificence of a rainbow or the fragrance of the air after a rain shower? Natural wonders help reshape our attitudes. What happens when we tune into our senses to recognize the world right around us?

Just a few weeks ago, I was reminded that what we see and feel or how we react is a question of perspective. My Hawaiian grandson, Chaison, was the messenger. I had heard on the national news that the Big Island was bombarded with wind and rain storms. Concerned about my son Robert and his beloved Kalei and their family, I immediately telephoned them. Seven-year old Chaison answered. "Aloha, this is Chaison."

I blurted out, "Are you all right? We heard about the storms."

Chaison responded, "Oh Grandma Geri, it is sooooooo beautiful!"

Chaison's joyful assessment left me speechless. He reminded me in that instant that all the wonders of Nature are ours to perceive. How we choose to look at Life itself determines our experience. Quite a Lesson from a Wise Child.

If the doors of perception were cleansed, everything will appear . . . as it is, Infinite.

William Blake

Ithaka

As you set out in search of Ithaka
Pray that your journey be long,
Full of adventures, full of awakenings.
Do not fear the monsters of old.
You will not meet them in your travels
If your thoughts are exalted and remain high,
If authentic passions stir your mind, body, and spirit.
You will not encounter fearful monsters
If you do not carry them within your soul,
If your soul does not set them up in front of you.

Written by Greek poet C. P. Cavafy and read at the funeral of Jacqueline Kennedy Onassis.

CHAPTER NINE

Springtime of Autumn:
Embracing the Seasons

*Let me stand in my age with all its
waters flowing round me.*
                    Margaret Fuller

*Winter is on my head, but eternal
spring is in my heart.*
                    Victor Hugo

*Live in each season as it passes;
breathe the, drink the drink, taste the
fruit, and resign yourself to the
influences of each.*
                    Henry David Thoreau

*Oh, give us pleasure in the flowers today ;
And give us not to think so far away
As the uncertain harvest; keep us here
All simply in the springing of the year.*
                    Robert Frost

A Shift in Consciousness

A new generation of mature seekers, receptive to spiritual truth, is now discovering Joel Goldsmith's teachings, which have lost none of their relevance, aliveness, and power. I foresee that those teachings will reach and impact even more people in the 21st century than during his lifetime.
Joel Goldsmith's profoundly inspiring books represent a vital contribution to the spiritual awakening of humanity.

Eckhart Tolle

I discovered a tremendous shift occurring in my own life on all levels—personal, professional and spiritual—in the 1970s. When I came upon the written works of Joel Goldsmith (1892-1964), I was intrigued by his invitation to move into another level of conscious awareness—to see through the appearances of "this world." I discovered that Joel Goldsmith's teachings had opened the hearts of people around the world and he was considered a modern mystic by many who encountered his works.

Then I learned that Joel Goldsmith's class tapes were being played each week by a quiet, unassuming elderly woman in Seattle. Myrtle Howe had attended many Goldsmith classes during his lifetime. She was committed to sharing his message with a small group who met in silence every Thursday evening at a downtown Seattle hotel just a mile or so from my home. When I learned of the possibility of hearing such recordings, I was curious. By then I had read many of Goldsmith's books but had never heard his voice.

Each time I attended those Thursday evening gatherings to listen to Goldsmith recordings, I found that I was lifted out of the chaos and challenges of every day life. I entered in silence and left in silence, as did others and I began to mysteriously experience a profound sense of peace. I did not understand what was happening.

A Contemplative Life

About that time, another "teacher" appeared in my life by sheer coincidence. I was beginning to see, however, that there are really no coincidences! Bee Culver dropped by my home with a neighbor one evening for a cup of tea. Bee, a tall, gracious white-haired lady, sipped her chamomile tea and expressed interest in my work in gerontology. She noticed two books I had written, *Healthful Aging* and *Joyful Aging,* and said she would love to read them. Of course I was delighted to give her copies. Almost immediately we were conversing with an openness of friends who had known each other forever.

Then Bee shared an experience that was so outlandish that I could only gasp at its significance. She told me that years earlier on a stormy night in downtown Seattle she and her husband were rushing toward their car when he reached down into the gutter and fished out a paperback book, shook it off and handed it to her. She thought it rather strange but rather than protest, she accepted the soggy book and dropped it beneath her feet on the passenger side of the car. They drove on home through a massive Northwest rainstorm barely able to see the road.

As they approached their brick home in North Seattle, the storm's toll was everywhere. Branches from the majestic oak trees lay strewn across the lawn, streetlights were out. Wanting nothing more than to get inside and light the fireplace, Bee decided to appease her husband by taking that book from the gutter inside their home. She tossed it under a heating vent thinking it would likely dry out or crumble. In either case, she thought "I will discard it later."

Little did Bee anticipate the impact of that rain-soaked book. "After about two days, I noticed the title *The Contemplative Life* by Joel Goldsmith—and I began reading—Geri, I stayed up all night reading!" "Suddenly I felt flashes of light . . . yes, yes, this is what I have always known I was seeking!" "But no one had ever spoken to me about contemplation in this way." And she added "that was the beginning of a feeling of peace and serenity I never dreamed possible."

Bee truly emanated peace. We remained close friends until her passing at age 91. Over the years, I saw her weather circumstances that would have been devastating to most. The sudden death of her youngest son, Jack, was a painful blow. Jack was jogging to his son's soccer game when he fell from an overpass onto the highway below. He died of the injuries just as Bee reached the hospital only to see what she described as "his broken body." In her deepest grief, Bee knew that Jack was more than his body.

Just months after Jack's death, I saw Bee consoling women whose children had died. Younger women seem to gravitate toward Bee for counsel and guidance. People she had never seen before often approached her in public places and poured their hearts out. She radiated a light that people of all ages seemed to recognize, a beholder of peace and serenity. But she rarely spoke of the Goldsmith teachings (sometimes known as Infinite Way teachings) unless specifically asked.

Shortly before her passing last July, Bee told me that she wanted to give me her collection of Joel Goldsmith books. Of course I was thrilled as she lovingly offered them to me. Now I have a treasure trove of Goldsmith books with Bee's handwritten notes in each of them. I am seeing more each time I open one of these books.

Her last note to me said:

Dearest Geri,
FedEx just picked up your box of Goldsmith
books. They are on their way to your home.
Hope they 'awaken' others as they have me
since the 70s. Thank you for all you contribute
to the joy of my life.
Eternal Love, Bee

Through her gentle demeanor, Bee Culver was a quiet teacher. I feel her presence and precious friendship each time I open one of my Joel Goldsmith books. They are treasures — daily reminders that we live in a world of Oneness.

Transcending Age Through Contemplative Living

Shortly before his passing in 1964, Joel Goldsmith designated five teachers, all of whom had been his long time students, to carry on his work. Virginia Stephenson is one of those five that I have the privilege of calling my friend.

I continue to gain new insights through classes and conversations with Virginia. Over the past ten years or so, she has patiently and lovingly answered the questions I pose. Thanks to light-filled Virginia, I began to look at growing older (in calendar years) as an opportunity to grow in spiritual meaningfulness. Her ageless and gracious countenance is a vivid reminder that opportunities for growth never end.

Through my conversations and correspondence with Virginia, I have had an extraordinary opportunity to ponder both questions and answers provided so generously by this remarkable Teacher.

As a gerontologist, I was intrigued by Virginia Stephenson's positive attitude about aging. On a recent occasion I asked, "Virginia, could we talk about some of your ideas and some of the teachings that led you to such a joyful look at aging?"

Virginia responded, "Maturing. That is the word. The word 'aging' never sounds right to me. The unfolding of consciousness is what takes place when we live fully. As youngsters we explore the physical world, and everything around us in the outer world. As time goes by, we become more interested in intellectual things. But there comes a time when we begin to inquire: Is there not something more than just the physical and intellectual? Is there not something else? We feel that there must be another dimension. We can almost touch it, but we do not really know what it is."

I asked, "How can we access this other 'dimension' that you speak of?"

Without hesitation, Virginia answered, "We learn to meditate . . . We start to look within ourselves for the treasure we have, the treasure of inner peace. A quiet walk, appreciation of nature, being grateful for the good we have already received, enables us to be receptive to this new dimension of unconditional Love."

Then she added, "We enter within to the silence of our own being, which is Consciousness."

I asked, "Do you see maturing as a period of transcendence?"

She responded precisely, "Well, the minute you discover this inner kingdom of love you begin to transcend the universal hypnotism that is operating in the world, which keeps people angry, restless, dissatisfied, irritable. When we find this Inner Resort, this resting place . . . we become more joyous. We have an Inner Resort that is the most refreshing, renewing, restoring activity you can ever imagine. All the health spas, all the massages, all the long hours of sleep cannot renew you as much as ten seconds of touching that Inner Resort of Love."

Your Inner Resort

When I asked Virginia to talk more about that Inner Resort, she said, "I think of a resort as a place where you rest your mind, where you stop taking thought about tomorrow or about yesterday, and you focus just in the *Now* moment. You rest from judging the appearance world."

She added, "The Inner Resort is a place of peace, joy, harmony."

Then Virginia began to refer to Eastern teachings as well. She said, "The word 'darshan' means inner peace. When you come into the presence of a person who has 'darshan' that 'darshan' embraces you. When you come into the presence of someone who is peaceful, you feel it."

I commented that I had often seen people drawn to my dear friend Bee and I think she embodied "darshan."

"Oh, yes, Geri," Virginia said, "when you come into the presence of someone who does not judge you or criticize you but recognizes that you, too, have this Inner Resort, you are pulled into that lovely atmosphere. This is called grace. This is practicing the presence of Love, and this is always a *Now* activity. Love is never in a hurry, because it is outside of time. Love is always Now."

"Would you please tell me about the work of your teacher, Joel Goldsmith?"

She smiled softly.

"Yes, Joel was my teacher. He opened meditation for me. Some of his books, such as *The Art of Meditation, The Art of Spiritual Healing,* and *The Con-*

templative Life are in seminaries of all denomina-
tions . . . Joel showed me that inspiration and new
ideas come from within. If you are living on the pe-
riphery of life, always oriented to the appearance
world, you will not have the inspiration that comes
from within."

When I asked why the Goldsmith work is sometimes referred to as the Infinite Way, Virginia said,
"Because it is a way of Infinity. You may read Lao-
tzu, the great Chinese philosopher, who shows us
similar thoughts in the *Way of Tao*. This is a universal message. In Joel's writings he deeply honors Je-
sus the Christ as the Way Shower which I do also."
She added, "The Buddha gave a great message as he
revealed the illusory nature of the appearance
world."

I asked Virginia to tell me about some of the writings of Joel Goldsmith, including letters he sent to
students which have recently been published in a
book *The Heart of Mysticism*.

"In his writings Joel explains the nature of illu-
sion; he calls it a universal mental projection. We
could call it a universal conditioning that we've all
grown up with from the time we were children."

She added, "Truth can only be found within your
spiritual consciousness. You have to turn away from
the appearance world and find truth within yourself;
then you will find that you see things differently."

I said, "Virginia, please tell me why you see problems as invitations to come up higher."

Without hesitation Virginia responded, "Problems
are really opportunities to grow in grace and under-

standing. So when a problem confronts us, we do not blame outer circumstances, and we do not blame people. We take the attitude: this is an opportunity for me to see the 'stone carved out of the mountain without hands.' That is a very beautiful mystical saying from the Book of Daniel."

She added, "Daniel was a prophet, and he saw 'the stone carved out of the mountain without hands'. Often the activity of the Spirit within us is called the Living Stone. So when we have a problem it is an opportunity to be a 'beholder' and watch the living stone work."

"The problem is not solved by might or power. Without effort, Love reveals the way or the solution. What does that say to you, Geri?"

Her question caught me by surprise and after taking a deep breath I responded: "Well, it says . . . anything is possible."

Virginia smiled and nodded. "Yes, Geri, that's right!"

Dealing With Compassion Fatigue

Virginia knows that I am continuously seeking ways to apply these teachings to my work as an educator of social and health service providers—particularly in my field of gerontology. How could this message help those who serve our elders? So I asked, "There are many health care workers who are in great despair these days, who are exhausted, who are what we call "burned out," or who are experiencing compassion fatigue. They work in nursing homes or other long-term care facilities and are seeing people in very sad circumstances. What's the main message for those who are experiencing a lot of difficulty these days?"

Virginia said, "Well I think that before they ever go to work, they have to enter that stillness within themselves, that Inner Resort, in order to be renewed and refreshed. The true sense of meditation is resting alertly, alive in a listening attitude, asking to be a transparency for Love. When you rest in that attitude, you are fed from within and renewed and restored."

She went on to say, "The great poet Browning said 'Truth is within ourselves . . . and we must open out a way for this hidden splendor to escape.' Meditation is the way."

She added, "There is a saying from the Sanskrit: 'Who is that single-eyed, pure-hearted soul who will look at me in the rags of a beggar and the sores of a leper and say: Son of God, I salute thee. Stand forth.' We must see everyone as a child of God."

Seeing Through Appearances

Virginia Stephenson invited me to awaken to another dimension of being. She reminded me that we are here to "see through appearances."

When my mother was making her transition from this earth plane, Virginia gently and kindly guided me in awareness and acceptance. I was at my mother's bedside continuously in those final days and I know that I grew in conscious awareness through the experience.

Virginia asked me to "look at what the world calls death in a spiritual way."

She said, "Geri, this is an opportunity to grow in awareness of the *I AM*. Changeless being is never born and never dies. The body is laid aside when it is no longer useful. We are guided through a door to a higher level of consciousness."

My friend, Elizabeth Harris, a hospice chaplain visited regularly and each time softly repeated this Unity prayer of solace and comfort for Mother.

> *The light of God surrounds us;*
> *The love of God enfolds us;*
> *The power of God protects us*
> *The presence of God watches over us.*
> *Wherever we are, God is, and all is well.*

I am grateful for friends in the caring professions who teach through their deeds and actions. Anne McKinley, a wise and compassionate social worker, and Karen Rader, an exemplary hospice nurse, also helped me see what the world calls death as the entrance to another season.

When the very insightful hospice physician, Sam Downing, came to the memorial service we held in Mother's living room, he spoke of seeing her passing as a lovely sunset. He said, "The nurses' reports on her quiet acceptance of her journey told me how much they enjoyed visiting her during the Autumn of her life."

> *In the Autumn of my life, let*
> *every leaf be shining gold.*
> Ann M. Gartrell

CHAPTER TEN

Circle of Life: Living Now

. . . Go forth, in every direction —
for the happiness, the harmony,
the welfare of the many.
Offer your heart, the seeds of
your own understanding
like a lamp overturned
and re-lit again
Illuminating the darkness.

The Buddha

Life is a full circle, ever widening until
it joins the circle motions of the Infinite.
Anäis Nin

Rest in the deep, clear well of content-
ment within you. Be at peace.

Joel Goldsmith

A Parenthesis in Eternity

Joel Goldsmith often referred to the present moment as a "parenthesis." Certainly our life on this earth plane is such a parenthesis—just a brief pause.

A Parenthesis in Eternity, one of my favorite Goldsmith books, offers an invitation to be fully present to the situations that enter our lives moment by moment. When we begin to recognize the essence of the present, we see more clearly the assignments given to us day by day.

Gaining awareness of this parenthesis within the circle of eternity is a step toward realization that life flows in circular motions. What then does this have to do with finding meaning and purpose in our lives? What about our *Search for Significance*? What could possibly be more important than this moment?

As we enter this world, we are dependent upon those who care for us. As our world expands, we begin to realize our own potential. We awaken to a new experience as we grow in consciousness awareness and the mysteries of our lives are revealed to us—a process of unfoldment.

Each stage of life is a stepping stone in preparation for the next, a continuous journey. Our choices and above all, our attitudes, shape the pathway.

I recently spoke with Virginia Stephenson about the significance of the Sanskrit words, *Look to this day . . . it is the very life of life . . . In its brief course lie all the truths and realities of existence . . .* Virginia reflected on the beauty of the moment, the beauty and essence of *Now*.

Then she invited me to read from her book *Genesis: Awakening from the Dream.* "The inward journey is not a journey in time and space but a change of direction inward to discover the spiritual capacities that each of us embodies. Few people have experienced the dynamics, the power, and the depth of their spiritual nature, but the fact that you have opened this book is an indication that you have been touched by the Spirit and you are journeying inward."

I asked, "Consciousness is a word that is being used very much these days, but do you think people have widely differing interpretations?"

"Well, I will just say what it means to me." Virginia responded. "Consciousness is total awareness—total awareness without a process. It is something that is always present wherever we are as we develop our Inner Ear. It's the fabric of existence, the fabric of being. Consciousness is universal; consciousness is infinite. It is available to all. It is omniscient; it is omnipresent; and actually it is omnipotent, the power that sustains the universe, including humankind."

She added, "We have what we call human consciousness, which is awareness of the mental and physical aspects of human experience. Then we have transcendental consciousness or spiritual consciousness which is awareness of the Soul. The Soul realm is a very familiar place to poets, artists, musicians, writers. Also to those who are interested in the planet Earth, who love the out-of-doors. Why do they love nature? Mother Earth is a Living Soul and we are fed when we go into nature and commune."

Virginia explained, "When we go to the mountains or the seaside, we are restored and renewed. However, we individually have access to the one Soul, which is spiritual consciousness. This is done in meditation when we are resting in silence."

I learned from Virginia's teachings and the many writings of Joel Goldsmith that, indeed, the faculties of Soul enable us to have compassion, an understanding heart, the ability to forgive, and to express gratitude. Soul opens us to the beauty of life.

In the Buddhist tradition this process is symbolized by the lotus flower arising from the mud. The lotus symbolizes purity, the underlying pure nature of human consciousness that Buddhists term "the true nature of mind." The mud symbolizes the limited nature of the unenlightened mind—our physical and mental desires and addictions, our afflictive emotions, our beliefs in sin, disease and imperfection, our propensity toward vengeful words and deeds when people and events upset us.

All the limited forms of the human aspect and the mental aspect are the mud. Out of the mud the lotus blossoms. As we learn to meditate we experience our own blossoming. This is where we find joy and a profound sense of fulfillment.

In Goldsmith's book *A Parenthesis in Eternity*, he sees one life as a circle of eternity. We live in a parenthesis in the circle of eternity.

When we meditate, we rise out of the parenthesis. We enter a new dimension. We can see life as a spiral—moving upward. The symbol of the lotus is about our consciousness blossoming and coming to fruition. It is about becoming all that we can be.

Virginia Stephenson has often said to her students "You can rise out of your earthly consciousness or awareness into the light because your Soul is who you truly are." Can you think of yourself as a lotus blossom? A lotus blossom becoming whole and beautiful and free?

Recently I came upon a tapestry greeting people entering a community library. I invite you to ponder it and add your own words. A simple reminder of the *Now*, it says:

Think freely.
Practice patience.
Smile often.
Savor special moments.
Make new friends. Rediscover old ones.
Tell those you love that you do.
Feel deeply. Forget trouble.
Forgive an enemy.
Hope.
Grow.
Count your blessings.
Observe miracles. Let them happen.
Discard worry.
Give. Give in. Trust.
Pick some flowers. Share them.
Keep a promise.
Look for rainbows.
Gaze at stars.
See beauty everywhere.

Be wise. Try to understand.
Take time for people.
Make time for yourself.
Laugh heartily. Spread joy.
Take a chance. Reach out. Let someone in.
Try something new.
Slow down. Be soft sometimes.
Believe in yourself. Trust others.
See a sunrise. Listen to rain.
Reminisce.
Cry when you need to.
Trust life. Have faith.
Enjoy wonder.
Comfort a friend.
Have good ideas.
Make some mistakes.
Learn from them.
Celebrate life.

Author Unknown

Lift up your eyes upon this day break-
ing, for you . . . give birth again to the
dream . . . Lift up your hearts. Each
new hour holds new chances for a new
beginning.

Maya Angelou

It seems to me that one of the most ba-sic human experiences, one that is genu-inely universal and unites—or, more precisely, could unite—all of humanity is the experience of transcendence in the broadest sense of the word.

Vaclav Havel

. . . when we have listened and looked deeply, we may begin to develop the energy of brotherhood and sisterhood between all nations, which is the deep-est spiritual heritage of all religions and cultural traditions. In this way, the peace and understanding within the whole world is increased day by day.

Thich Nhat Hahn

CHAPTER ELEVEN

Inner Vision:
Cultivating Discernment

When living out from the Center of Being, you are untouched and nothing acts upon you because you do not react to the world of appearances.

Joel Goldsmith

Out beyond ideas of wrongdoing and right doing, there is a field. I will meet you there.

Rumi

The secret of strength lies in the Quiet Mind . . . If you will be steadfast on the path to which your feet have been guided, you will find the treasure of life — a never-ending stream of help and healing . . .

White Eagle

Discover the World Within

How do we retain an inner coherence in a world filled with contradictions? How do we discern a voice of authenticity, a voice with heart? Aren't we all seeking to be authentic and follow that inner voice?

Not too long ago, I turned on the television set and saw Elizabeth Gilbert, bestselling author of *Eat, Pray, Love* being interviewed by Oprah Winfrey. When I tuned in I heard Elizabeth say, *"Entrances are everywhere—we all need stillness every day . . . sacred moments of silence . . . honor and celebrate yourself."* And then she said, *"Every person you meet is a teacher."* I immediately perked up and remembered the words that Viktor Frankl shared so many years ago: *"Listen to the person in the street. He or she will be your teacher."*

My heart quickened when a young woman in Oprah's audience spoke up.

> *"When you discover the world around*
> *you . . . you also discover the world*
> *within you."*

Ah! Yes, yes!

The following morning I went out to purchase *Eat, Pray, Love* and with my reader's eyes and active imagination began journeying with Elizabeth in search of herself through Italy and India. But when she reached Bali, I felt transported there with her!

To my delight Elizabeth Gilbert took me back to Bali, that magnificent tropical Indonesian island I had twice visited. And to my astonishment, as I read of Elizabeth's ride on the back of a motorcycle on a winding tropical path, I realized she was going to see a healer I visited with Budi, my guide in Bali. An uncanny sensation of familiarity came over me.

I could not believe it was the same healer who had made an indelible impression on me. Almost instinctively, I reached into my closet that holds treasures from my travels. There rolled in a cardboard tube for safekeeping, was the signed ink drawing I had purchased from Ketut Liyer, the Balinese healer, on the day of my visit to his home. As I looked for photos we had taken on that memorable day, I recognized the courtyard and all its gracious and intricate details that Elizabeth relates in her book.

I remember that Ketut Liyer (through Budi's translation) told me he is a descendent of nine generations of medicine men. At the time, I had an irritating rash on both arms that I seemed to get every time I exposed my skin to direct sunlight in tropical climates. I had developed this photosensitivity in Guyana, South America, a decade earlier when I had an allergic reaction to an anti-malarial medication called Fansidar. I was told by skin specialists that nothing could be done about this recurring rash. "Just stay out of tropical sunlight," the dermatologists cautioned.

So I asked Ketut Liyer (through Budi) if there was a remedy for the rash on my arms. He immediately reached up to the rafters of his home which held hundreds of carefully rolled scrolls from those nine generations of medicine men. He pondered momentarily as he looked at me again and carefully selected two scrolls. He very deftly unrolled one scroll that I presume dealt with dermatology remedies. And then he proceeded to mix a potion that he directed Budi to tell me to apply several times a day. Within two days the rash disappeared and did not recur. I was impressed.

My visits to Bali were extraordinary. The first time I went with a team from the United Nations Development Program to work with health care providers evaluating educational programs being offered in Balinese villages. This particular work assignment during the months of September and October,1997 also took me to the islands of Sumatra and Java in Indonesia as well as to Thailand. As with all the international work, there was the "work inside the work" and lessons to be learned from teachers along the way.

Bridge from Soul to Cell

Dr. Joyce Hawkes, the acclaimed author of *Cell Level Healing: The Bridge from Soul to Cell* had been my friend and teacher (yes, I have had many teachers!) for well over ten years when I went to Bali. As I went about the world doing my health education work, Joyce often spoke to me about the *"work within the work."* She, too, was aware that our greatest lessons come from the most improbable sites and teachers.

I often consulted with Joyce before my international assignments to such places as Brazil, Paraguay, Guatemala, Mexico, Honduras, Dominican Republic, Grenada, Antigua, Macedonia, Swaziland, Uganda, Kenya, Lesotho, Jordan, Australia, New Zealand, Japan, and other places where I was invited to work on global health issues.

Joyce is a compassionate listener and she helped me interpret and accept my assignments. She also helped me overcome any semblance of hesitancy I might have had about traveling to unknown places. It was Joyce Hawkes who reinforced what I had known for as long as I could remember—that we all have unique work to do in this amazingly interconnected world. My work is global, cross-cultural, and cross-generational.

When I met Joyce in Seattle during the early 1980s, she had embarked on studies of indigenous healing practices. Only a few years earlier Joyce was a scientist committed to the pursuit of knowledge through quantitative and verifiable means. She had no interest in spiritual matters until one day while dusting her mantel, a leaded glass window fell onto her head. She remembers the impact of the blow to her head and said, "Suddenly reality shifted, and I was no longer confined to my crumpled body on the floor."

Joyce told me that she found herself in a place of perfect peace and love and light. At first she discounted the experience as "hallucinations," but she quickly became aware that she had access to another dimension of consciousness that would impact her life thereafter. Shortly after the near-death experience, Joyce left her university career as a biophysicist and set about working with indigenous healers in the Philippines, South India, and Bali where she explored uncharted territories that linked biology and spirituality.

133

Dr. Joyce Hawkes teaches that emotional, mental, and spiritual experiences can have a profound impact at the cellular level. She taught me many things, but above all, she showed me that appreciation of the gifts we bring into this lifetime is essential for fulfilling our unique life journey.

Joyce said that after her near-death experience, she lost her fear of death and along with it her fear of separation from the Source. She also lost any notion that the Source is available to only the few who belong to a specific religion, sect, or geographical or cultural identity. "The healing presence of the Source is for everyone," Joyce maintains.

Her many trips to Bali over the course of a decade absolutely fascinated me. I was especially interested in experiences Joyce had as she worked with healers in their villages. She told me that Balinese healers are expected to bridge the physical and spirit realms to obtain information for the patient and his or her family. They often prescribe an herb, healing water, a ritual, or advice on an emotional issue that can bring peace to a troubled individual.

Joyce's primary Balinese teacher and mentor was a woman of late mid-life. Jero Mangku Srikandi was considered a master healer with great skill in linking the dimensions of consciousness. Joyce described Jero as a woman of imperturbable demeanor and a profoundly loving spiritual connection.

When I was invited to work with the United Nations team in Thailand and Indonesia, I phoned Joyce to ask for more information about Bali. She graciously gave me the name and phone number of I Wayan Budiasa (Budi) who had served as her guide and interpreter over many years. And she told me Budi would be able to take me to meet her mentor, Jero Mangku Srikandi.

After our teamwork was completed and the reports had been submitted to the United Nations office in New York, I arranged to return to Bali on my own time to meet Budi and learn what I could.

I Wayan Budiasa

Budi received me with the graciousness that is so integral to the Balinese culture. But little did I know that Budi was a cultural historian whose wealth of knowledge would so enrich my stay. I later learned that Budi is considered the top guide in Bali, having served in that capacity for numerous prestigious institutions. I also learned that Budi was the primary source of information for *Sekala* and *Niskala* a two-volume book series on Balinese culture.

Not only did Budi take me to spend a day with Jero Mangku Srikandi but he interpreted the rituals she performed and introduced me to the people of her village. Budi told me about his own experiences with Balians, Bali's traditional healers. Budi said, "I saw my first Balian when I was a young boy. I used to watch people go to him and receive treatments. This elder looked at what kind of illness the person had and then made an herbal medicine. Whenever I became sick with a headache or a fever, I would ask him to cure me. He always gave me the right kind of medicine."

So, with Budi's assistance and an introduction to Jero Mangku Srikandi, I was invited to observe her work with clients and to personally experience her healing practice. She explained to me, through Budi's translation, that she is connected to the healing consciousness of Buddhism, Islam, Hinduism, and Christianity. Jero said simply, "Spirit works through me to help others. When people come to me with a problem, my job is to release the problem so that the person's life becomes peaceful."

Jero explained, "I never went to school. I became a Balian when I was seven years old. I have been helping people ever since." Then she added, "Spirit tells me about the people who come here for help. When a patient comes to me, I am guided to know what is wrong and what kind of medicines will help. When Spirit dances me I feel like I am flying. I am very light. I am the only Balian who dances like this. If I am told to move my hands, my hands instantly move."

Without my asking for anything, Jero began dancing and chanting. As she swiftly danced around me I felt a soft gentle breeze. When she stopped she sat beside me and told Budi to tell me "not to worry; you will continue your global work for a long time. And your health is good."

Then Jero brought a bucket of water that Budi told me had been blessed. She invited me to drink from the cup she held in both hands. After I sipped a bit of the water, she poured the entire bucket over my head and body. I was wearing a loose blue rayon skirt and blouse that day and the entire frock was pasted to my body as if I had been caught in a sudden rainstorm. But I was in such an "other-worldly" state that I was unconcerned. Budi took my camera and photographed me sitting under a huge gnarled banyan tree immediately after the experience. It was blissful. When I look at that photo today, I can still feel the peace of the moment.

The next day Budi took me to see Ketut Liyer, the artist and healer who cured my rash. And then Budi invited me to his own home in Jimbaran and showed me the books on Balinese culture compiled by Fred B. Eiseman, an American with whom he had collaborated for over ten years. Eiseman in his attributions wrote, "there is literally not a paragraph in this book that is not a direct result of Budi's help."

Budi and I talked about discernment and our universal quest for deeper understanding. He helped me see the essence of his beautiful and beloved Bali. And he spoke about some of his extraordinary teachers and way-showers. He also talked about his experience of collaboration on written works that are introducing ever-increasing numbers of people to Balinese culture.

When I left Bali enroute to Singapore, Budi came to the airport in Denpesar. As we said farewell, he gave me handwritten note with a message he said he wanted me to remember. It said:

> *"Saraswati is the goddess of knowledge in Bali. She is the wife of Brahma, the Creator. She is always depicted standing on or next to a holy swan. The swan is consecrated to be holy, as along with its*

brethren—the duck, the swan ferrets out its food from the mud and can distinguish that which is edible from that which is murky and dark (mud). This is another analogy for the quest for knowledge. Ducks and swans can also live in two worlds; the world of water and the world of earth."

I Wayan Budiasa from Jimbaran, Bali

Turtles for Peace

As I concluded a workshop on "Caregiving" at the last World Congress of Viktor Frankl's Logotherapy in Dallas, Texas, a silver-haired gentleman of slight build made his way slowly to the front of the room and offered me a gift—a tiny turtle carved from rose quartz that he carried in a soft tan leather bag. He said simply, "I cannot travel far these days so I give these turtles to people who will take them wherever they go in the world."

I marveled at the beauty of the rose quartz and thanked him for the lovely gift. He said, "These turtles are making their way around the world slowly but in good time." Then he quietly stated, "I gave one to Archbishop Desmond Tutu. I call them *Turtles for Peace*."

That *Turtle for Peace* reminds me each day that all of us are called to break from our shells of fear and to birth a more soulful way of being. We are called to create a more harmonious way to live and to open our hearts to unfoldment *Today* and *Each New Day*.

Precious gifts come to us in most unexpected ways, seen and unseen. Who calls you to open your heart? What do we fear and why? Is it fear of being misunderstood? Or rejected? Or reluctance to get involved? What is happening in our world today? Can we be *Turtles for Peace?*

Turtles are found on every continent of the world. In South America, the Amazon people believe that the turtle is resourceful and knows how to emerge safely and victoriously out of any challenging circumstances.

That gentleman in Texas is gently reminding us through his *Turtles for Peace* that we are called to be part of a planetary shift. The shift to a purposeful and significant life is calling us all.

The World is Waiting for You

"The world is waiting for you to find your voice"
James O'Dea

Apollo 14 Astronaut Edgar Mitchell founded the Institute for Noetic Sciences (IONS) after an extraordinary experience on his way back to Earth from the Moon. Mitchell felt the separation of mind, matter, and spirit dissolve in an experience of oneness.

As a well-trained scientist, Mitchell knew that someday science would come to fully understand the wholeness and interconnectedness that he experienced in a flash. But he knew that first we would have to learn how to access deeper levels of human consciousness and to understand the powers of heart and mind that reach beyond a purely rational framework.

Edgar Mitchell knew that shifts in consciousness would be required to create a sustainable and peaceful planetary society. He founded the *Institute of Noetic Sciences* for that purpose. Its mission is to explore the frontiers of consciousness to advance individual, social and global transformation.

James O'Dea, current president of the *Institute of Noetic Sciences* speaks to our universal longing today. He says:

> *"When we understand the potential within each human being, we will wake up to the importance of developing the inner life. In every age, mystics, sages, and teachers have shown us how to go deep within and, by doing so, experience the great gift of awareness itself. Listen to the voice within. The world is waiting for you to find your voice."*

Everyday Divine Encounters

I heard the British scholar, Karen Armstrong, speak in Seattle to a large group of people from varied ethnic backgrounds about world faith traditions. Her comments touched me deeply.

A cloistered Roman Catholic nun for seven years, Armstrong, embarked on a search for meaning by exploring world religions while emerging from deep despair and depression in her post-convent years. Today she is an acclaimed author and scholar. She found her voice.

Karen Armstrong recounted the story of Rabbi Hillel, who said: "The whole of the Torah can be summarized by 'That which is hateful to you—do not do to others.' The rest is commentary. Go study."

Armstrong went on to explain that the golden rule is found in every major religion of the world, "Do unto others as you would have them do unto you—or don't do to others what you would not want done to you." She said, "Discover what gives you pain; do not inflict it upon another. Any interpretation of scripture that leads to hatred is illegitimate. Unity of the entire human race depends on love of God and love of Neighbor. Every scriptural interpretation must lead to compassion and charity."

As I sat listening to Karen Armstrong that evening, I jotted some notes, "See the Divine encounters every day. Honor the stranger. Recognizing the Holy otherness of the stranger can give us an awareness of transcendence. A vision of the Divine is what we see when we acknowledge the stranger at our gate."

To unfold one's truth within oneself is the lifelong aspiration of every human.

Rabindranath Tagore

Empty your mind of all thoughts.
Let your heart be at peace.
Watch the turmoil of beings,
But contemplate their return.
Each separate being in the universe
Returns to the common source.
Returning to the source is serenity.
If you don't realize the source,
You stumble in confusion and sorrow.
When you realize where you come from,
You naturally become tolerant,
Disinterested, amused,
Kindhearted as a grandmother,
Dignified as a king.
Immersed in the wonder of the Tao,
You can deal with whatever life brings you,
And when death comes, you are ready.

Lao Tzu

CHAPTER TWELVE

Grace and Gratitude:
Being Present

There is no better way to thank God for your sight than by giving a helping hand to someone in the dark.

Helen Keller

As we express our gratitude, we must never forget that the highest appreciation is not to utter words, but to live by them.

John F. Kennedy

One cannot help but be in awe when he contemplates the mysteries of eternity, of life, of the marvelous structure of reality. It is enough if one tries merely to comprehend a little of this mystery every day.

Albert Einstein

We are in a moment of grace . . . unprecedented awakening to our relationship to the universe.

Thomas Berry

As I looked through the papers on my desk after presenting a seminar at the University of Washington, I found a handwritten note that I treasure. To this day, I have no idea who left it. The essence of that treasured message is:

> *We give thanks*
> *Thanks a million times over*
> *For those people those rare,*
> *precious, marvelous people*
> *Who have found a secret place*
> *And pitched their tents there.*
> *Those who dwell in attitudes*
> *Of hope and confidence.*
> *Who reach across rather than down,*
> *Those people whose presence*
> *Always leaves us*
> *Feeling better about ourselves.*
> *We give thanks for these*
> *Loving people,*
> *These beacons for the unfoldment of Love.*

I often share these words in my workshops and seminars. And I invite the participants, nurses, doctors, administrators, social workers and others, to breathe deeply and ponder the significance of being beacons for the unfoldment of love in our world.

There was a time when we were discouraged from speaking of the transcendental nature of life in academic circles. Today I find people everywhere are hungry for a message of hope, a message that allows us to embrace one another with understanding and acceptance.

Healthcare and social service providers are flocking to hear uplifting messages that are being brought forth today by an ever-increasing number of people who are finding their voices.

Remember the *Turtles for Peace*? There is great longing for the peace, the justice, and the dignity that is the birthright of all. More and more of us are called to participate in the shift in consciousness that is now palpable.

Have you felt the shift? In the midst of change, challenge, and even chaos we are called to experience a new dimension of consciousness. We are called to go into the Silence where we are One with the Source. That is the invitation! As Virginia Stephenson says:

". . . every problem is really an invitation to move to a higher level of awareness."

The Legend of the Praying Hands

The legend behind the Praying Hands by Albrecht Dürer—two hands in prayer—is a beautiful source of solace for many. I have found that there are multiple versions of this legend, so symbolic of the gifts of grace and gratitude.

About 1490, two boys, Albrecht Dürer and his younger brother, were struggling young artists in Europe. Both worked to support themselves while studying art. Work took so much of their time that progress on the artworks was very slow. They reached an agreement one day; they would draw straws and one of them would work to support them both while the other would study art.

Albrecht won and went off to study, while his

brother worked in the mines at hard labor so that Albrecht could immerse himself in the art world. They agreed that when Albrecht finished his apprenticeship, he would then support his brother who would be able to realize his own dream to study art.

As the world now knows, he had not only talent but also genius. When he had attained success, he went back home to keep his bargain.

Albrecht soon discovered the enormous price his younger brother had paid. Sadly, as the younger man did hard manual labor, his fingers became stiff and gnarled. His slender artist hands were ruined and he could not longer create fine art work. Though his dreams could not be realized, instead of becoming embittered he indeed rejoiced in Albrecht's success.

One day Albrecht Dürer came upon his brother unexpectedly and found him kneeling with his gnarled hands intertwined in prayer. Albrecht, hurriedly sketched the folded hands of his beloved brother and later completed the masterpiece known simply as the Praying Hands.

Today museums and galleries around the world feature the magnificent genius of many of Albrecht Durer's works of art. And his praying hands continue to tell an eloquent story of love, sacrifice, labor and gratitude.

Gift of Love

The Praying Hands symbol hold special meaning to people in twelve-step programs such as Alcoholics Anonymous, Overeaters Anonymous, and others. The praying hands are found on plaques, wallhangings, stone carvings, and sundry other places the world over. They are a silent acknowledgement that out of the darkest days comes hope.

A young woman I knew and greatly admired for her commitment to a spiritual path over many years, once told me, "Yes, I am proud of all the progress I make day by day working my twelve-step program in AA." She continued, "but I was so consumed with resentment toward my father—some days it was more rage and resentment than I could bear!"

This extremely competent healthcare administrator had grown up in what she termed a "colossal dysfunctional family."

She said, "It wasn't until I made a trip back East to visit the family gravesite that I could let go." In a tearful voice she added, "Standing alone at the cemetery under a willow tree, I looked at the headstone on my father's grave. Even though I had attended his burial service years before, I was not aware of the symbol on his gravestone: Dürer's Praying Hands. My years of resentment and the weight and angst of carrying that baggage suddenly lifted." She went on to say, "I felt an immense release of the burden of unforgiveness–and my heart began to soften"

Do you know anyone saddled with baggage of the past? What have you observed?

Look Around . . . Teachers Abound!

Think of Meister Eckhart's words:

"If the only prayer we ever say is 'thank you,' that will suffice."

Look around. Teachers abound! Remember the person on the street. Who have been your teachers? What are their gifts that warrant a thank you? Often we do not recognize them until years later when we have the "gift of hindsight."

Grace and gratitude are attitudes we can cultivate. Look around Today. Breathe deeply. Go into the Silence. Learn to endow even a few moments of each day with Love.

Viktor Frankl walked with a reverence for life, a gentleness that was palpable yet indescribable. His life work focused on helping people find meaning in their own lives regardless of circumstance, age, or social condition. Most of all he advocated "Giving as a way of Being."

The last time I saw Dr. Frankl was in April, 1989; he was the keynote speaker at a conference attended by more than a thousand gerontologists in Washington, D.C. Viktor Frankl, then in his eighties, with diminishing eyesight that led to complete blindness, spoke directly and passionately to our hearts with a timeless message of unconditional meaningfulness throughout the life span—a message of awakening and awareness of the gift of each new day.

A vast potential for growth exists within each of us regardless of what is swirling all around. The invitation is to walk with serenity one day at a time.

Come, come, whoever you are,
Wanderer, worshiper, lover of leaving.
It doesn't matter.
Ours is not a caravan of despair.
Come, even if you have broken
your vow a thousand times.
Come, yet again, come, come.

Attributed to Rumi

To pray for the world means to look
out as if seeing this globe of the uni-
verse in front of you, and feel your
hands or your love going out around
that globe . . . Hold that globe in a
whole armful of love, understanding,
forgiveness . . . never think of victo-
ries, think of Peace.

Joel Goldsmith

Sign On - Just for Today

Invest in this Day

Go Within and Listen Deeply

Neutralize Negativity

ACKNOWLEDGEMENTS

"The best and most beautiful things in the world cannot be seen or even touched ... They must be felt with the heart."

Helen Keller

Heartfelt thanks to my Teachers and to my Global Family who have all helped awaken me to a path of purpose and meaning. Over the years my students, colleagues, friends, family, and neighbors have taught invaluable lessons that I gratefully acknowledge. Each and every encounter has held a lesson—often recognized only in retrospect.

Special thanks to Sam Horn for expert guidance and especially for encouraging me to "write on!" Sam's gifts of perceptive listening and crystallizing ideas have made all the difference. My heart is filled with gratitude.

John and Shannon Tullius, founders of the Maui Writers Conference, provided an extraordinary opportunity for me to experience the joy of writing in a nurturing community.

Drs. Robert and Dorothy Barnes and Dr. Ann Graber and the International Board of Directors of the Viktor Frankl Institute of Logotherapy have embraced my global work. I am indeed grateful for the honor of being a Lifetime Member of the Institute.

Many thanks to Kate Robinson, my editor whose vision and genuine interest in *Search for Significance* made it a joyful experience.

To my husband, Roberto, and to our sons, Robert Peter and Ethan David, thank you from the bottom of my heart. Grace and Gratitude ...

Geri Marr Burdman
July 2008

RELATED READINGS

Angelou, Maya. *Even the Stars Look Lonesome.* New York: Random House, 1997.

Armstrong, Karen. *A History of God: The 4,000-Year Quest of Judaism, Christianity and Islam.* New York: Ballantine Books, 1993.

Baldwin, Christina. *Storycatcher.* Novato, CA: World Library, 2005.

Barks, Coleman. *A Year with Rumi.* San Francisco: Harper Collins, 2006.

Brokaw, Tom. *Boom!: Voices of the Sixties.* New York: Random House, 2008.

Brokaw, Tom. *The Great Generation.* New York: Random House, 2004.

Burns, Ken. *The War: An Intimate Story, 1941-1945.* New York: Knopf, 2007.

Butler, Robert N. *The Longevity Revolution: The Benefits and Challenges of Living a Long Life.* Jackson, TN: Perseus Books, 2008.

Butler, Robert N. *Why Survive?: Being Old in America.* Boston: The Johns Hopkins University Press, 2002.

Chopra, Deepak. *Peace is the Way.* New York: Random House, 2005.

Dyer, Wayne. *Change Your Thoughts: Change Your Life.* Carlsbad, C A: Hay House, 2007.

Eiseman, Fred B. *Bali, Sekala and Niskala.* Hong Kong: Periplus Editions, 1990.

Eisler Riane and David Loye.*The Partnership Way*.
Brandon, VT: Holistic Education Press, 1998

Erikson, Erik and Joan. *The Life Cycle Completed*.
New York: W.W. Norton, 1997.

Frankl, Viktor E. *Man's Search for Meaning*. Boston:
Beacon Press, 2006.

Frankl, Viktor E. *Recollections: An Autobiography*.
New York: Perseus, 2000.

Frankl, Viktor E. *The Doctor and the Soul*.
New York: Second Vintage Books, 1986.

Frankl, Viktor E. *The Unheard Cry for Cry for
Meaning*. New York: Perseus, 2000.

Frankl, Viktor E. *Man's Search for Ultimate
Meaning*. New York: Basic Books, 2000.

Gilbert, Daniel. *Stumbling on Happiness*.
New York: Random House, 2007.

Gilbert, Elizabeth. *Eat, Pray, Love*. New York:
Penguin, 2007.

Goble, Frank. *The Third Force, The Psychology of
Abraham Maslow*. New York: Grossman, 1970.

Goldsmith, Joel S. *The Thunder of Silence*.
New York: HarperCollins, 1993.

Goldsmith, Joel S. *A Parenthesis in Eternity*.
San Francisco: HarperOne, 1986.

Goldsmith, Joel S. *The Art of Meditation*.
San Francisco: HarperOne, 1990.

Goldsmith, Joel S. *The Contemplative Life*.
New York: Carol Publishing Group, 1994.

Goldsmith, Joel S. *The Heart of Mysticism,* Camarillo, CA: DeVross, 2007.

Graber Ann V. *Viktor Frankl's Logotherapy.* Lima, OH: Wyndham Hall Press, 2004.

Hawkes, Joyce Whiteley. *Cell-Level Healing: The Bridge from Soul to Cell.* New York: Atria, 2006.

Horn, Sam. *What's Holding You Back?* New York: St. Martin's Press, 1997.

Isay, Dave (Ed.). *Listening is an Act of Love: A Celebration of American Lives from the StoryCorps Project.* New York, Penguin Press, 2007.

Kelly, Mary Olsen. *Path of the Pearl.* Hillsboro OR: Beyond Words, 2002.

Kennedy, Caroline. *The Best Loved Poems of Jacqueline Kennedy Onassis.* New York: Hyperion, 2005.

Klingberg, Haddon Jr. *When Life Calls Out to Us: The Love and Lifework of Viktor and Elly Frankl.* New York: Doubleday, 2001.

Koerner, JoEllen G. *Healing Presence: The Essence of Nursing.* New York: Springer Publishing, 2007.

Kornfield, Jack. *The Wise Heart: A Guide to the Universal Teachings of Buddhist Psychology.* New York: Bantam Dell, 2008.

Kübler-Ross, Elisabeth. *Death, the Final Stage of Growth.* Englewood Cliffs: Prentice Hall, 1975.

Luskin, Fred. *Forgive for Good.* New York: HarperCollins, 2004.

Mandela, Nelson. *In His Own Words.* New York: Little, Brown and Co., 2003.

Maslow, Abraham. *The Farther Reaches of Human Nature.* New York: Viking, 1971.

Moyers, Bill. *Fooling with Words: A Celebration of Poets and their Craft.* New York: Perennial, 2001.

Pattakos, Alex. *Prisoners of Our Thoughts: Viktor Frankl's Principles at Work.* San Francisco: Berrett-Koehler Publishers, 2004.

Pizer, Marjorie. *Selected Poems,* Sydney, Australia: Pinchgut Press, 1984.

Shriver, Maria. *Just Who Will You Be?* New York: Hyperion, 2008.

Shriver, Sargent. *Point of the Lance.* New York: Harper and Row, 1964.

Sorenson, Ted. *Counselor: A Life at the Edge of History.* New York: Harper Collins, 2008.

Stephenson, Virginia. *Genesis: Awakening from the Dream.* Lakewood, CO: Acropolis Books, 1997.

Tolle, Eckhart. *A New Earth: Awakening to Your Life's Purpose.* New York: Dutton Press, 2005.

Tutu, Desmond. *No Future Without Forgiveness.* New York: Doubleday, 2000.

Williamson, Marianne. *The Age of Miracles: Embracing the New Midlife.* Carlsbad, CA: Hay House, 2008.

Zukav, Gary. *Soul to Soul: Communications from the Heart.* New York: Free Press, 2007.